Rural Voice

A Greenwood

Rural Voice

Tales from the
Upper Dale
Nidderdale

Recorded, edited
and compiled by
A Greenwood

HALFWAY HOUSE
PUBLISHERS

RURAL VOICE

Published by
Halfway House Publishers

Typeset by
4 Sheets Design & Print Limited

Printed by
ImprintDigital.com

ISBN 978-0-9932274-4-8

Typesetting and printing funded by
Friends of Nidderdale
AONB Countryside Fund

Contents

Rural Voice

Nidderdale Man

The genuine Nidderdale Dalesman is a tall, athletic personage, with considerable length of limb, plenty of bone and muscle, but not much inclined to corpulency. His countenance is fair, generally florid, the freshness of the colour being retained even to old age with great strength and agility. Though not so quick witted and wide-awake as the inhabitants of large towns, they are shrewd and intelligent, kind and sociable, and almost everyone with characteristic peculiarities of his own, distinct from those of his neighbour; not drilled into a dull uniformity by the influences of an useless civilisation, speaking more freely their genuine thoughts and feelings with little of duplicity or crooked cunning in their disposition; their general uprightness of conduct is beyond question.

William Grainge, 1863

Map of Upper Nidderdale
showing the villages and narrators

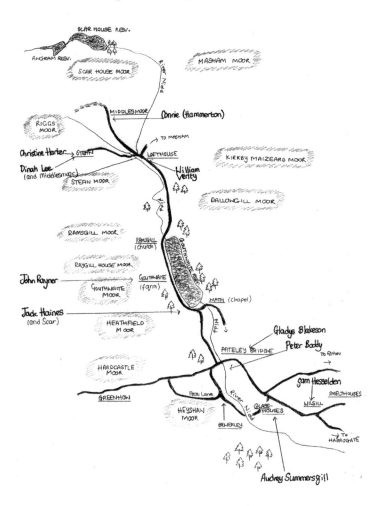

© Anna Greenwood

Introduction

This book began as a personal journey into the landscape that surrounded me through the people that live in it and shape it. An incomer to Yorkshire, I chose this part of the world to be my home after travelling around some of the poorest, remotest parts of the globe. It was in those places that I witnessed the simplicity of life when the clutter of modernity was stripped away. People lived, loved and died in a place without record and without trace. It was this simplicity and tradition that captured my imagination, and took me up into the nearby dale of Nidderdale, to its remote, wide open expanses, and to the people who had made it their home.

I undertook this with little training and a lot of persistence. Since the beginning of the project, I have trained in oral history methods and improved on what was a bumpy start. The recording equipment I used improved in quality from a hand held MP3 player (now obsolete) to more sophisticated dedicated recorders that afforded a better sound quality.

I spent my time in various locations in the Yorkshire Dales, recording the stories people told me. I approached them as a stranger and I left as a friend, often with tea and cake inside me. Their stories are so much more than I have written here, and we spoke about much more than I recorded. At times, I shared my story too. In this book I focussed on a group of people who share a common area. However, if you were to take out the place names and replace them with those of another dale, the stories would hold true. These are stories about being human, and that is their common language.

We are all driven by a desire to connect, whether to ourselves or to other people, to landscape, cultures or traditions. This basic desire to connect to the traditional and the simple is what drove this work for me, and the result is a collection of experiences from the people who lived them, in their own words. I think that point is particularly important — that these stories are in their own words. I am the story collector.

These are not my stories. These are the memories, thoughts and feelings of the individuals who lived them.

Narrators

While predominantly contained within the Upper Dale of Nidderdale — the part that extends north of Pateley Bridge on the road to Middlesmoor — there are also contributions from narrators living outside of this area but still within Nidderdale. These were retained as they refer to people, places, and experiences that are common, and because the narrators were established personalities in their own rights.

The narrators themselves, and their families, were significantly touched by two world wars. Their whole way of life was affected in so many ways. Warfare brought hardships and shortages. It affected the landscape and utilised its resources. But, the wars also brought work and generated a community spirit the likes of which we have never seen since.

A note on the transcriptions

The words in this book have been transcribed from recorded conversations and edited for clarity. Many of the hesitations, repetitions, and verbal tics have been removed for ease of reading. Where hesitations have been left in, they are represented by three dots ... to indicate the narrator's pause. In many cases, responses such as laughter have been given in brackets to indicate the emotional context in which the words were spoken. A style of local speech, or dialect, has been used where it does not hide the meaning of the spoken words. The name of the narrator is also given **in bold** at the start of their words.

Where my own speech is recorded, it is written *in italics*.

Many of the transcripts are available in part to listen to on a CD that was released in 2017, *Rural Voice. Tales from the Upper Dale: Nidderdale*, compiled by Anna Greenwood. Universal Product Code 6-43157-44227-1.

'A full belly and a roof over your head is never enough of course. People dream and find solace and inspiration in many different ways among the flower-filled meadows and wind-swept moors of the Yorkshire Dales.'

Karen Griffiths
Interpretation Officer
Yorkshire Dales National Park Authority

THE FOLLOWING POEM was written by Louis de Bernières about the fading pagan gods of Greece, and it appears in his collection *Imagining Alexandria*. 'The miracle period is over,' writes de Bernières in his introduction. '... young Greeks want to wear baseball caps and play the electric guitar ... Greeks took up reading pulp fiction ... They no longer knew what it was like to have lived through a war or dictatorship ... I do not know what is going to happen next.'

The same can be applied to Nidderdale. The language, people and stories held in this book are fading from memory and being replaced. The old ones will pass away and their names will be consigned to carvings on headstones in graveyards. Stone houses and chapels lay ruined in abandoned hamlets. Fields are no longer cut by hand. Local dialect is falling out of use. The availability of entertainment and an increase in leisure time have altered the dale's character, turning it into a place to visit rather than a place to live. Local business men and women turn from farming to the more profitable tourist trade, and with that comes new language and new stories. Each generation brings its own views on life, and that is as it should be.

But we do not forget the old stories, nor do we forget the old ones who spoke them. We recall them, record them, and read them still. That is the purpose of this book.

Many of the transcripts are available in part to listen to on a CD that was released in 2017, *Rural Voice. Tales from the Upper Dale: Nidderdale*, compiled by Anna Greenwood.
Universal Product Code 6-43157-44227-1.

The Old Ones

We cut down the groves
And made fires and beams for our houses.
Of the golden sickle
We made bracelets and rings
For the boxes of the Christian ladies.
We take the stones, and some we broke
For our walls;
Others we built into churches.
We lost the means of reading runes,
There was no more writing on feast days
In token or in true.

There is no memory of any of it now.
We put it behind us, convinced by new stories,
Exotic languages,
Yet more extravagant mysteries.
There was incense, candles and bells,
And the irresistible offer of hope.

But the old ones have by no means gone.
It is still this island that they love.
It is we who are remembered
At those times in spring or autumn,
Midsummer or winter,
When their ever-youthful souls stand wistful,
Holding hands
In the shade of long-demolished groves.
Sometimes, indeed, a vigorous shadow
Vaults a stream or
Leaps from the crown of hills.

by *Louis de Bernières*
from *Imagining Alexandria*

The Narrators

Rural Voice
Part One

Narrators:
Audrey Summersgill
Christine Harker
Connie Bickerdike
Dinah Lee
Gladys Blakeson
Jack Haines
John Rayner
Peter Boddy
Sam Hesselden
William Verity

MANY OF the older Dales folk are related to each other and have lived in the area for generations. Their way of life and language are inbred, and similarities in practices can be seen from one farming community to the next across the Yorkshire Dales and into the Lake District. It is a way of life that has been handed down, and written about by many authors. It is a way of life that Beatrix Potter sought to preserve, that Hannah Hauxwell lived – or endured – in relative solitude, that James Rebanks captured in 2015 in *The Shepherd's Life*, and that William Hudson captured a century earlier in his book *A Shepherd's Life*. Considered a classic at the time of its publication in 1910, Hudson's *A Shepherd's Life* was an account of the lives of those who lived on and worked the land in nineteenth-century rural Britain – tales of sheep dogs, farmers' wives, poachers and local fairs recalling a sublime account of a way of life that has largely disappeared. That way of life is disappearing across the country, not just here in Yorkshire.

Hefted

JAMES REBANKS, in his book *The Shepherd's Life*, lays out the definitions of the word 'Hefted'. It is a word I first heard used by hill farmers in Nidderdale, but have since heard it used across the north of England.

HEFT Noun:
1) (*Northern England*): a piece of upland pasture to which a farm animal has become hefted.
2) an animal that has become hefted thus.

Verb: *Trans.* (*Northern England and Scotland*) *of a farm animal, especially a flock of sheep*: to become accustomed and attached to an area of upland pasture.

Adj.: Hefted: describing livestock that has become thus attached

Sheep are hefted, or 'hoofed', to the land they're born onto. There is something inside the lamb that links it to the place of its birth, and urges it to return there. Sheep brought down from the moors will hang around at the moor edge of a field, seemingly wanting to get back to where they belong, no matter that they might be on much finer grazing.

My own life is more itinerant, moving from the place of my birth, the Home Counties, to Yorkshire in the mid-1980s, then on to Manchester, London, back to the Home Counties, and back to Yorkshire. I also spent time in Asia for months at a time over a period of several years. Through all that change, my father's voice told stories of growing up in the place he belonged to, in rural Norfolk, where he worked on the land until he himself became 'educated'. Education was his ticket out, although I sometimes wonder if he ever felt completely at home in his new environment. As he aged, he kept alive the memories of the rural ways and freedom of his younger years. He recorded events in his own writings, and the stories took life through home movies, capturing the movement – if not the sounds – of characters that he grew up with. It was this looking back, this nostalgia, that piqued my own interest in what seemed to me a much simpler way of life.

I know that is just a romantic pastoral idyll. The hardships and poverty of that time countered the seeming simplicity with which the people went about their lives. And yet a part of me yearned for a time and place without Smart Phones and Internet, and a time when there was no need to know something *Instantly*. Conversations passed the time, and developed the family bonds and closeness, weaving the shared threads that ran through the generations.

Back to Yorkshire and the Dales, and as I met with these people I listened to their stories with curiosity about what it would be like to have stayed in one place a life time – to be hefted. There is a barn on one of the properties that is known as High Barn – up the hill from the farm house and closest to the sheep on the moors. It's where they store the hay for winter feed, and where the cows were once bedded down. Carved into the faded red paint on the huge, arched, dry wooden door are initials. I imagine men – and I'd like to think women also, although I doubt it – standing beside the barn talking about their fathers' initials, and talking about their fathers' father, before carving their own names and thus making their own mark of the moment. Initials on barn doors; births, deaths and marriages written in church records; common names. These are all parts of stories that blur across the generations.

The Hill Farmers

The town folk and the hill farmers live different lives from each other. In the Dales the people are shaped by the land that surrounds them, by the work that they do, by a community of shared tasks and by their stories. To raise a family or to run a farm means finding someone like-minded with whom to share your life. As a young farmer grows up and looks for a wife, he may yearn for the lights of the city, but settle for a woman who can work with him in the life-long business of farming.

John Rayner spoke of wanting to meet up with the girls of Harrogate who seemed to know so much more about life than the girls of the Dale. In the end he married a farmer's daughter and together they raised a family and ran the farm.

William Verity married John's sister, and lived further up the Dale from the Rayners. Both families farmed with their children 'Up Dale'.

John Rayner

'*When were you born, John?*
Thirty-two. Nineteen thirty-two.
Aye. You're reckoning up how old
I am, aren't you! (Laughs)
I am! I've worked that one out.
And then I got married about,
what, late fifties, and we've four
sons. Four lads. There's three of
them now, but Our John got
educated, and went to Oxford
University and learnt German and French and all that, and he's
married a French girl, so he's abroad like. We've two or three lads
at home. Matthew, youngest, he got educated, he went to Norwich
University, East Anglia, and then Leeds, and studied all sorts, and
then he couldn't get a job so he's ended up here like.
Your grandfather came down to Gouthwaite?
From Lofthouse. He married daughter down in Gouthwaite Hall.
Carling they called them. It's a well-known name, in't it. Carling.
And he married... in 1890 or so... and took over from Mr Carling.
Took over and started farming, down in reservoir in 1891. But in
1898 they started building this reservoir and flooded him out, and
they lived in that house for two years, in this end, cos this end were
under water, and that end he lived upstairs for two years until they
built this. Do you see? This was sort of underwater. They pulled it
down in summer when it were dry, you see. He had t' live in this
end for two years upstairs with kids and his wife and they built some
steps down at back and he farmed this land till they rebuilt this, so
he came t' live here didn't he. It's all same stone. Same windows.

William Verity

'When were you born, William?
Thirty three.
John's one year
older than me.
John Rayner.

A SENSE of belonging comes from being born into a place, but that sense can also come to those who were born elsewhere and moved into the area. The place may not be their origin, but over the years they come to think of it as home. All bar two of our narrators were born in Yorkshire's Nidderdale in the early part of the twentieth century. Some were born into a particular line of work, such as farming or engineering, naturally taking over from their parents. Others left Nidderdale to train at their craft – often pushing their parents to the limits of their finances to fund their education – and returned later to work in the area.

The Child

CONNIE BICKERDIKE (née Hammerton) moved into the Dale with her parents as an infant and stayed there until her family left when she was ten years old. As with many families at the time, it was work at Scar Dam that brought them to the area. Labourers came

from across the country and from Ireland to join a temporary village of workers' huts, a school and a shop that grew around the works.

I met Connie at her home in Milton Keynes and although her well-spoken voice is full of Southern vowels, she has strong memories of her time spent growing up in this remote part of Yorkshire. Her childhood was a time of village shops, Sunday school lessons, freedom to explore the fields, and foraging. The children around her were farmers' children, and their lives revolved around the farms, each other, and the annual events in the village. Connie moved into the area as a very young child.

Connie Bickerdike

'I can remember where I was born, which was in Goole. I was born in Goole.

And you moved to Scar?

Yes. We moved up there for my father's work, because they started on that in '21, the Scar Dam. They started that in twenty one. Well, I wasn't born until '23.

The Gamekeeper

OUR GAMEKEEPER moved from Scotland and followed in the footsteps of his father. Responsible to the land owners, he managed the moorlands and the stock of birds needed for the shoots. It is gamekeepers, invisible to people who pass through or take their leisure in these areas, who shape the moorland landscape. He is the second of only two of our narrators who were born outside of Nidderdale. Following his long service award and his retirement, he remained in Nidderdale with his wife.

Gamekeeper

'I was born in 1940. Sixth of September 1940.

You're from a line of gamekeepers? Your father was a gamekeeper?

My father was, yes.

And did it carry on before your father?

No. No. Grandfathers were farmers. They were farmers. And then, 2005 when I retired, I had the pleasure of my long service medal presented at Pateley Show, which I think was probably the first time it ever happened.

How long was that?

40 years. 40 years of service.

The Business Man

THE HESSELDEN family name is seen throughout the Dale. It is one of those family names that, like the farmers, is hefted. The agricultural and farm contractor business that Sam Hesselden set up after the war continues to thrive today under the guidance of Sam's son from their home in Wilsill. During the Second World War, Sam worked for War Agricultural Executive Committee (WAREC), which was the start he needed to set himself up in what became the family business when the war ended. Events during the war had a huge influence on his life, alongside music, the church and his family. Sam told me his story in 2012, four years before he passed away.

Sam Hesselden

'I was born at Burnt Yates down the road — about four or five mile away where those humps are in road. I was born there on a farm, where me father were working on a farm, just on outskirts of village. I had one brother and three sisters. And we were born at Burnt Yates, the whole lot of us.

Me birthday's at thirtieth of March – next to thirty first of March.
I were born in '25.

The Teacher

AT THE TOP of the Dale lies
a cluster of houses near Middlesmoor in a place known as
Stean. Like many Dales villages there were once shops
and a Post Office in Mid-
dlesmoor, and also in nearby
Lofthouse. Stean was on the
outskirts of the village – a mile away on foot over the fields – and
although Middlesmoor was the nearest 'centre', people were often
self-sufficient and relied on buying, selling and bartering to live. Children walked to school, as I did in my own childhood.

Dinah Lee was born in the hamlet of Stean. From there she moved
to Middlesmoor, then studied in Ripon before returning to Middlesmoor. When we spoke she was living in Pateley Bridge some eight
miles from Stean.

Dinah Lee

'I was born in Stean, so I haven't moved far, have I! (Laughs) I walked
to Lofthouse school at first until I was nine. My father died when I
was three and my step brother continued farming but he never
enjoyed it. And then we moved to Middlesmoor to live with my
grandmother and so I went to Middlesmoor school after that, latterly, and then I went to high school, yes
That was the one in Ripon?
That was the one. Girls' High school
Where you were boarding?
I was a weekly boarder, which was nice. We used to go on a Monday

morning and come back on a Friday night. It was good because you had the best of both worlds. You still had your home life and your home links as well as being away. My boys had to board and they went to the Ripon Grammar school, but they weren't allowed home except half term and once in between. They weren't allowed home for weekends and in some ways you lost the links with them and you weren't able to be as interested in what they were doing as if they'd been just off for the week. But I mean it worked out alright. It did them good in the end.

The Postwoman

ONE OF THE very memorable Dales characters was Gladys Blakeson.

She had many jobs and, although unable to read and write at first, learnt and took on the role of Post Woman at Middlesmoor.

She let nothing get in her way, and remained full of energy and life. In 2016 Gladys Blakeson celebrated her 89th birthday. The following year I was pleased to be invited to her 90th party, and later to a Christmas party at which she had been tasked with organising the party games. It was an entertaining evening of pass-the-balloon, bingo, quizzes and a knobbly knee competition.

Here she speaks about when she was born, and how she remembers the date.

Gladys Blakeson

'And you were born in nineteen thirty seven?'
Twenty seven. I wasn't born until 1927. I'm 88 now. I'm 89 in September. Pateley Show. I allus remember me birthday. Pateley Show weekend.

The Engineer

JACK HAINES was born at Scar where his father worked as an engineer on the building of the dam. His grandmother used to move from place to place with a hostel that could be taken down and moved on the railways. At Scar, she no longer needed the transportable hut so she moved into one of the Scar bungalows and ran a hostel from there. Jack Haines passed away in 2017 and his ashes were scattered at Scar.

Jack Haines

'When were you born, Jack?'
I was born at Scar, Scar Village. 18 The Terrace, Scar Village, 1926.

The Labourer

PETER BODDY was a man of few words. He passed away a couple of years after this interview. We met at Pateley Bridge Methodist Church. Peter worked with his father at Greenhow extracting fluorspar from lead waste.

Peter Boddy
'I were born in 1929, Love. December 20th 1929.

The Farmhand and The Seamstress

AND FINALLY we have two more narrators to listen to whose dates of birth are not recorded. Audrey Summersgill, born at Bewerley, worked on the family farm and turned her hand to relief milking. Christine Harker born at Stean works as a seamstress, and still lives in Stean today.

Audrey Summersgill
'I was born at Cliff Cottage, just on bottom road between Glasshouses and Bewerley. Cos my dad and my uncle farmed in partnership on that farm that's right on that road side if you go on that bottom road, this side of the outdoor centre. We had a kitchen... there was a bit of an extension on it, it was what we used t'

call the wash house, and the coal house. Just the kitchen and a bit of a pantry, two main rooms and the lounge downstairs, and then upstairs, two main rooms and a bathroom. There was a little tiny box room off my mum and dad's bedroom. I can remember getting electricity, but we always had water.

Christine Harker

'My granddad got a farm in Stean in 1932 and farmed there and turned it eventually over to me dad who was their only child. He was Fred Harker. Me granddad was John William known as Jack. My youngest brother is now on the farm. They went there as tenants in 1932 and in the 1940s they were able to buy it. It became available to buy. I don't know whether they paid it off in instalments or what really. They wouldn't be spending a lot of money out and about. Mostly people stayed quite local to the area. I mean, my granddad was church warden at Middlesmoor for 40 years. He was in the British Legion and was a Parish Councillor. They didn't have the time to move about. Everything was more work related. They spent the day going from one place on the farm to the other. The leisure time would be going to church.

Rural Life

Rural Voice
Part Two

Rural Voice

The Beginning

Photo: (Anna Greenwood) Sam Hesselden with one of his tractors

The Beginning

WE HAVE all heard stories since we were children, and some of us have told stories to our own children. Every story starts with a beginning and grows from there. Some of the narrators in this book wondered whether their stories were of interest beyond the Dale. Others, such as Sam Hesselden, had thought about writing his own history himself. Here, we let Sam introduce us to what follows:

Sam Hesselden

I was gonna write a book meself on me life story of Nidderdale and what went on. I think the best way to do, start at beginning because it's so ... so interesting. Now then, alright, I'm starting now from scratch (laughs)...

over the tops :
the (usually more direct) route over the high moors between
dales.

*Me grandfather ... and a lad called Harry Graham worked together
all over, they walked over the tops, started work at Scar, from
Leighton over the moor.*

Rural Voice

Reservoirs

Photo: (Peter Boddy) Peter Boddy with his father, Scar House Reservoir

Reservoirs

IT TOOK eight years to build the dam at Gouthwaite – construction began in 1893 and finished in 1901. This allowed the water authorities to ensure a flow of water to residents and mills along the River Nidd further down the valley. Once Gouthwaite was built, work could start on Angram and Scar to provide water to the Bradford area. Construction at Scar was completed in 1933 and it was officially opened in 1936. It is one of the deepest reservoirs in England. The Nidd Valley Light Railway was constructed to enable the reservoirs at Scar House and Angram to be completed. The railway opened in 1907 and closed in 1937.

Jack Haines

They had t' build Gouthwaite first to guarantee the mills a supply of water so they weren't gonna take it all and the mills had nothing to run on, so they had t' build Gouthwaite first.

My father was an engine driver. He was working at Leighton, Leeds reservoir, and he heard me grandfather – that was his father – was general foreman, and him and a lad called Harry Graham, worked together all over, they walked over the tops. Started work at Scar. From Leighton over the moor. There was a few people lived about there. There was some houses buried under the reservoir. Farms. Little farms. Yes. That's how me father got in.

Then me dad was asked to go to Silsden reservoir, and there were some pumps there to pump water back to Addingham, and they couldn't get them... and me dad was a fantastic engineer. They asked 'im t' go. He was boss of Scar in them days. So he went there... no, he were at Gouthwaite then, so I took his job over. Owd Renton said, 'You take his job.' So I was at Gouthwaite. Aye, and I worked at that job till I went to the army. I went to the army on my eighteenth birthday. We were in France when we were eighteen.

Photo: (Ann Smith, Anna Greenwood) One of the original Scar bungalows, moved to Shepherd's Lodge Farm near Brimham Rocks (1) circa early 1970s showing original front door and asbestos roof, (2) 2017 with new roof and added porch.

Gladys Blakeson

My grandparents came when they were building Angram as a young married couple and they lived in one of them wooden chalets that they had. They had these wooden places and so many people in 'em, hadn't they. And of course 'e got a job driving one of the engines up and down the valley with all of the materials. It wasn't the one where the people got in. It was for the materials, and it used t' have t' sometimes help the big engine up the incline, you see, pushing it.

Jack Haines

You know there was hostels at Scar, A to K? Well, my grandma 'ad one of those, but long before she came there from Newport and all over, she had a hostel she could take in bits and put on the railway and they went wherever the big jobs were, and so when I was at Scar, she didn't need it you see cos they were all built, so she had, what, eight daughters, and they all worked for her, but me mother didn't work for her. Me mother worked for Newlands that were chief engineer up at the Old Scar House. Gone now. It was pulled down. Aye. The Old Scar House was there for, God knows, generations, long before. And there's a reservoir buried under Scar. A little reservoir called Haden Carr; a little reservoir there that was sending water to Bradford, and that was buried under Scar. The thing was, to be quite honest, it was the mills – they needed an awful lot of water for wool washing. And when Bradford was booming, they really wanted more water. It was drinking water, but the thing to get it built was water for washing wool.

Went to school at Scar, there were three classrooms. Well, they ended up they had to send for a temporary classroom in those days, and we had Scar reunions, and we had fifty ex-pupils.

Dinah Lee

The railway line went up the bottom of the valley up from Lofthouse, up the bottom of the valley, up there. It missed Middlesmoor. All these people used to work up there.

Gladys Blakeson

The railway line to Scar came past the playing ground at Lofthouse school and he used t' blow the whistle. You know Sykes Bank where the big 'edge is at that 'ouse and you come up it? There was a railway went up the bottom you see and a bridge as he were passing the main road 'e used t' have t' come across the main road where that iron bridge is coming up to that farm, West House, and it went up the valley at the side of the river and then over another little bridge near Lofthouse. That's where the railway went. And, you know where the station house is as Lofthouse? There used to be a big boiler thing there and 'e used t' stop and fill up wi' hot water. And then the line came out over the end and over that bit of a bridge and then into Scar where the gate is, up that way. The side of the road was the railway line. There's the main road, and then like a banking isn't there. That's where the railway was.

We went up one day and me uncle, that's their youngest, was showing us where the foundations was for this bungalow. It was sort of up on the moors on side of the wall coming down off the moors and it was there and the work at the bridge is 'ere, just looking across at it, and he worked on that, and then of course first world war broke out, so his oldest boy and me granddad went to war, and he'd only be a young man then though wouldn't he. And of course when it was all over, he got this cottage in the village and lived there, and he used to help the landlord at the pub do his garden.

Dinah Lee

There was an old village hall up near where the car park is, a big wooden one there. It came from Scar, one of the huts, and that was used for everything until it... well, it was falling into disrepair. The children had their school dinners in there, and all the events were held in there. And inside the old, you see, there was this old stove at the end for heating. And then...oh it would be when school became empty... it was an opportunity for them to have a better hall. So that was what happened. It was quite spacious and there was a big billiard room, and they put covers on the billiard table and they used to use it for concerts and rigged all sorts of old sheets and things behind! (Laughs) Oh dear! The fun we used to have.

Photo: (John Rayner) Gouthwaite Hall before the reservoir flooded it.

John Rayner

He married daughter down in Gouthwaite Hall. 'Carling' they called them. Matthew Carling's daughter. Carling. It's a well-known name, in't it. And in 1890 or so he married this Harrogate Carling. Took over and started farming, down in reservoir in 1891. That's what this valuation is in there.

In 1890 when me granddad were farming down there, it were all grass, and there were footbridge across the river, straight opposite there. Now you've t' go down t' bridge and across. They've even closed that, haven't they.

But in 1898 they started this reservoir, didn't they, and flooded him out, and they lived in that house in this end, cos this end were under water, and that end he lived upstairs for two years until they built this. Do you see? This was sort of underwater. They pulled it down in summer when it were dry, you see. He had t' live in this end for two years upstairs with kids and his wife and they built some steps down at back and he farmed this land till they rebuilt this, so he came t' live here didn't he. It's all same stone. Same windows.

Dinah Lee

There were three shops in Middlesmoor once upon a time. But now there aren't any, you see. But that was probably when they were building Scar. There were a lot of navvies, or people, working at Scar, and it provided a lot of employment for local people. So of course there was more money about. I mean a lot of them used to walk to Scar every day to work and back, over the top. Over the moor or along the edge. Yes, so you see, it would be quite, I won't say wealthy, but there'd be much more money going the rounds. And navvies, there were navvies there you see. They were people that came to work when they were building Scar, and they were people, very often Irish, who used to travel from these building areas. They used to go from one to another. That's how they made a living. And then they would send their wages back to their families in Ireland. My uncle and aunt had the post office for quite a while and I know Aunt Hannah used to say at the end of the week, you know, Friday or whenever they got their money, she said they were coming to get postal orders, things like that, to send their wages back home.

navvy (noun) :
a labourer working on a building site, excavation, etc..
Shortened from navigator

There were a lot of navvies, or people, working at Scar ... They were people that came to work when they were building Scar, and they were people, very often Irish, who used to travel from these building areas. They used to go from one to another. That's how they made a living. And then they would send their wages back to their families in Ireland.

Rural Voice

The Price
of Things

Photo: (Gladys Blakeson) Showing sheep at Pateley Show

The Price of Things

MONEY HAS always played an important part in life, perhaps more so now than in the past when people didn't travel and there was little to spend it on in the remote parts of the dales. With farming, annual income cannot be predicted. Earnings are dependent on the weather, animal health and external events outside of the farmer's control. As a consequence, costs of items bought in such as straw also change from year to year. Once, families farmed small amounts of land to support themselves. Today farms are much larger, and fewer in number.

Selling Up and Moving

Dinah Lee

It was 1939 we decided to finish. We went to live in Middlesmoor, mother and I. But I always remember mother saying that at the sale there was not much money about and it was a very poor time really to sell up and I always remember her talking about a sheep dog that went for six pence. A good dog. A good working sheep dog and it was sold for six pence, and I have somewhere in an old notebook she kept the price of what she used to sell. Her eggs. And she used to make butter. I don't know if she made cheese, but she used to make butter.

Where would she sell that?

I don't know really whether Wrays the grocers...? I don't know. I don't think she would sell it at the door because not many people went up in that area at all, not as many as you get now. You get a lot more walkers, but in those days there were very few.

Which part of Stean was the farm? I know How Stean Gorge.

Well, you go further up the narrow track and it's only a hamlet. There'll be, what, about eight or nine little houses up there. And we were on a farm which was just on the right and they had all the land around it. It was still in the village, but maybe just a field or two out of it.

What is it now?

It's still a farm. No. It isn't, I'm wrong. The land has been lent off to another farm you see. They were rather small units in those days, but now they need a bigger unit to make them profitable, so the land has gone to another farm, I think they bought it, and it made their area larger. They were quite small units then. I think people must've had quite a struggle to make... well, they made a living, but it wouldn't be a very good living, profitable. But you see, as I say, to a certain extent you were self-supporting. Had our own milk and our own eggs, and a pig, you see, which they killed each year.

Wages

Dinah Lee

When you moved, which part of Middlesmoor did you live in?

I lived right bang in the middle. There were three cottages and Granny had the middle one and we went to live with her. We went in the spring and I think she died in about the June. She didn't live very much longer after we went. But she let my mother have the house so that she had security. She wanted to make sure that she had somewhere to live, so she left her the cottage.

Did your mother stay there?

Oh yes. Yes. She stayed there.

What work would she have done?

Well, she just had to go out cleaning and one time she was caretaker of the school, and an elderly couple she used to go bake for them, and you know she just had to make money where she could. I mean, we never had much money at all, but you didn't miss it.

John Rayner

And three of your four lads, they'll carry on in farming?

Yeah. Well, they seem to like it. Our John, he's on big wages and all that, he's an international accountant, and he says our bits of money's nothing! Compared to what he deals with. Millions. Japan and Middle East. These bankers' bonuses… what do you do wi' a million pound? What do you do with it? There's only one house you want at once, isn't there.

It's too much. Ought to be spread over more folks. What do you do with it? You can only eat three meals a day can't you and wear one set of clothes. And I have a friend, a nurse in Harrogate hospital, and she sees 'em dying every day. She says there's no pockets in a shroud, she tells me that all time, they've to leave it behind, haven't they.

Cos, up 'ere, farmers, as one fella said, 'I don't make much money, but there's nowt t' spend it on up here!' There's one fella, when electric came at first, you know, there's a bulb up there in't there, came in 1930, he only had one bulb and when he went into next room, he screwed that out and took it wi' him. Do you see? Aye. Saving money. Now they leave lights on all over.

When our John comes from Germany, never enters his head to switch a light off. It's using money, isn't it? With the heating on, and our lads complain. Cos he's got spoilt with money, you see (laughs). You ask Spencer Ewebank about money and he'll tell you. He knows what hard times are up there.

Jack Haines

There's some Americans down from where I used to live at Bouthwaite, and I used to walk my dogs down there and one came out once. He says, 'We've been talking at the Base about you lot in the war.' I says, 'Aye.' He said, 'We were saying how much were you paid?' I said, 'Twelve and six.' He said, 'you got twelve and six and hour?' I said, 'No we didn't.' He said, 'You got twelve and six a day?' I says, 'No we didn't.' And he says, 'You're not telling me you got twelve and six a week?' I said, 'We got twelve and six a week, we got a ten bob note and half a crown, and if you got killed they charged you for the blanket they buried you in.' He said, 'I don't believe you.' I said, 'I don't give a bugger if you believe me or not. I know what I got.' It's ridiculous, isn't it? That's what we got.

Paying for Things

Dinah Lee

My mother had quite a struggle when I went to the High school, with uniform and things like that, but boarding was free, so that was a help. A taxi used t' come up and take us up to Risplith and then there was a school bus run into Ripon from there. Picked us up, took us to school, and it was the same coming back on a Friday. But there wasn't just me, there was a group of us you see, she would have so much to pay towards this taxi that ran... Unless the County provided it...? They might have done. I don't know. I can't remember really. But, I mean, there was... well, there was quite a few of us from Up Dale went. We all went and boarded at Ripon because that was the only way you could get any further education.

Connie Bickerdike

A lot of cooking was done on the open fire in pans. When I look back it must've been expense because we had to have our pudding before the meat, and the whole object would be you'd be full with your pudding so that you wouldn't need much meat. I always remember that.

Sheep and Cattle

John Rayner

A lot of folk have sold cows; there's no pay at 'em. You're keeping a cow for a year for one little calf and there just in't much pay at 'em. Buying cattle cake and silage costs a lot. Straw we've to buy. Me granddad and me dad used t' always get bracken off moor for bedding cos you couldn't buy straw then. There were no transport, were there.

They ought to have bedding, for cattle inside, and now we've to buy straw and it's awful price. It's eighty pound a tonne, coming from Ripon, you know. And there's no pay at that, you see, is there.

Photo: (Anna Greenwood) John Rayner at Gouthwaite Farm with a new calf, 2016

Mechanisation hasn't necessarily made things better for farming.
No, not on hill farms. We have a four wheel drive bike you know, for going to moor on, and Colin, one of lads is going to change it to diesel. It were costing 'im six hundred pound in petrol just in one month to run this four wheel drive bike. But now they've made a diesel bike and we can fill up out of tractor diesel — red diesel — you can't use it on road, can you. But it's half price, so he's thinking of getting this bike next week. But petrol's gone through roof, hasn't it.

Six hundred pounds a month. That's a lot of miles you cover.
Well, every day, feeding sheep in winter and lambing time and all that carry on.
What kind of sheep?
Swaledales. Them wi' horns on. You've seen 'em, haven't y'? This (photo) is one from Pateley Show. Way back in seventies. They're making thousands now, tups like that. We've two friends Up Dale, above Middlesmoor, last year they sold one of them for £50,000. We can't beat 'em now at Pateley Show. They've gone t' top. Proper sheep. We're well down now.

Back in the seventies, if you got a thousand, that were top. We were given about a hundred for ordinary ones. They've gone through roof, prices. Pedigree men. Fella from Derbyshire bought this fifty thousand pounder, and if that tup on some good sheep gets a few tups worth ten thousand each, he's got his money back, hasn't he. But it's a risk. Cos 'e might not get one good enough. Well, it's happened many a time. It's same wi' race horses or anything, isn't it. A winner doesn't get a winner does it? No.

The Future

John Rayner
What do you think the future is for farming now?
Well, the last two years have been good for prices. You see, in 1991 first of all disease were BSE, you've heard of that, haven't you? It showed 'em on telly, an owd cow staggering about, didn't it. Well, it put people off eating beef completely, and they blamed cattle feed, didn't they. Well, we 'ad it and they never had any cattle feed. It wur just summat inherited in their brains. And now it's all died out, hasn't it. There were BSE, then Foot and Mouth ten years ago, or eleven. You couldn't sell anything. We were locked in. You couldn't sell 'em cos they had it in Dallowgill and had it at Grassington hadn't they, so they closed all up. Then there were Blue Tongue a couple of years

ago. Closed all auctions. And now there's another disease coming, a big long word, I don't know what it is. Sheep mainly, and cows. Lambs and calves are deformed when they come out. Started down South. It's in paper now, like. But farming were bad then, but now prices have gone right up. Mind you, costs have.

Straw's doubled in price. Fertiliser used t' be just over a hundred pound a tonne, now it's three hundred. Three hundred. And costs have gone up. Oil, everything. So we're no better off. No, no better off. But Government have started a scheme now, they're paying us for trees and walls, keeping 'em in good order on moorland and that, they're paying us a subsidy. A new scheme started. We haven't got anything yet, like. Trouble is, once you join this scheme, you can't do as you like. D'you see? You can't drain. They tell you whether you can drain on moor or kill bracken or do things. Y'have t' put tillage on meadows and that so as flowers grow. But their idea is t' cut stock t' half instead of trampling all flowers and live off subsidy, don't you see. But farmers like to farm as they want, don't they. Mow fields when you want to. Up Swaledale, they can't start mowing meadow way into July and sometimes it starts raining all back end, don't it. June's a fine month sometimes. So, it's a bit of handicap in't it. We've many a mile of walls and we've always kept them up, ever since they were built. Every time a gap falls, we build it don't we. A lot of farmers let 'em go down didn't they. And now they're paying grants for 'em to wall 'em. They're for shelter, aren't they, walls, on hill farms.

wrecken (noun) :
the hook for hanging the kettle on beside an old fireplace.

Me mother allus put kettle on wrecken first thing in morning.

Rural Voice

Life in the Village

Photo: (Connie Bickerdike, centre) Family photo outside Middlesmoor

Life in the Village

VILLAGES LIE *alongside the River Nidd and tucked into folds of land up and down the length of the Upper Dale. Wath, Gouthwaite, Bouthwaite, Ramsgill, Lofthouse, Stean, Middlesmoor, Angram, Scar, Lodge. Some of these names no longer relate to villages, but instead are known as reservoirs and ruins. Many villages had shops, butchers, schools, churches, post offices, public houses... but today the main shops and services are in Pateley Bridge. Life revolved around the family, the church, the pub, and the village shop. Produce was often local or home grown. And everybody knew each other.*

Shops

Photo: (Christine Harker) Middlesmoor Post Office

Dinah Lee
The village life itself, there's the church in Middlesmoor, the school, there's the pub as well. Has there always been a pub there?
There's always been a pub as long as I can remember. It was quite a small one to start with, you know, there was a back bar and things like that. But they've extended it. There were quite a few cottages on

that row and gradually they've taken them over and extended, made the pub area bigger and things like that, so that has grown. There was always a shop and a post office at the end. In fact, there were three shops in Middlesmoor once upon a time.

I can remember going to the shop in Middlesmoor and you bought a little bit of cheese, or you bought a pound of sultanas or currants, you know, things like that. And milk. There was always somebody in the village that sold milk.

Not pasteurised?

No, but we all survived! (Laughs)

Connie Bickerdike

We had to have a jam jar, and you took your jam jar to Mrs Walker in the shop and she must've had a barrel or a big container with a tap on it and you got your jar filled with Golden Syrup and that was it. No lids, nothing fancy like that.

You take it home open?

Yes.

Were you tempted to put your fingers in it?

No, I don't think we were. No.

Gladys Blakeson

Mr Oddie's shop... the building was just the same as it is now apart from they've got a door at that end but we used t' go into the front door and turn into the shop on the right. But now they go in at the other end and turn left into the shop. They've altered it.

What sort of things would he sell?

Oh, everything that you wanted. He was a proper shop. The Village Shop that sold almost everything that you wanted. And now there's nothing. All gone. Shut up and that's it.

Connie Bickerdike

Woodbines. I think most of the smokers up there smoked Woodbines. Woodbines were little cigarettes and they were only in a paper sleeve. They weren't in a packet like most cigarettes, but they were done up in little packets of five.

Dinah Lee

Wrays... there isn't a Wrays in Pateley now, but it's where the Milk Mart was. They were like a general store, but they used to travel, and I can remember them coming... someone used to come and take Mother's order, you know, what she wanted. It was things like sugar and tea, all that sort of thing, and they would come and take her order, and I remember they came with a horse and cart from Pateley, delivering with this horse and cart, and then they got a Big Brown Van, and they used to deliver with a Big Brown Van. And at Christmas you always got a box of chocolates, or a box of toffees, or something as an extra present. Those days have gone.

Connie Bickerdike

The joiner's shop, up at the end of the village, and the funeral director, made the coffins and all, and we could go and stand and watch them, and we were never in their way. In fact, we were often given the job of sweeping up the sawdust.

Christine Harker

The things that people in a town take for granted are be being able to pop out to the shops or pop out to see their friends, or services like the Internet. Do you use the Internet?

I'm on the point of getting connected up. I know one or two that a year or two ago were working from home, but it was a problem. We seem to have a lot of power cuts and they got quite upset about it because they were working the whole country really, so it was a problem.

When you were younger, how did you do your shopping?

Well, there was a post office and shop and another shop in Middlesmoor when we were children and there was a post office and shop in Lofthouse and the majority of the people did their shopping there at those shop. They didn't travel to a supermarket...well, there wasn't supermarkets then, was there. And on Wednesdays, Weatherhead's butchers came up with a van. Thursdays, Len Raw came up. He was another butchers in Pateley. Haig and Backs, the bread people... Oh and at one time we had somebody with green groceries. Most people had a vegetable garden as well and were quite self-sufficient.

Me granddad was the butcher in Lofthouse before he came to Stean and he took it over from Mr Thackray whose family had been in the butchering trade in Lofthouse for generations.

Where was the butcher's shop in Lofthouse?

When you go up past the car park, you know where you turn to go up to Masham where it curves round. It was built onto the back of a cottage. It wasn't connected.

Is that the picture we saw (page 65), with just an open window with meat hanging in it?

Yeah. That was when me granddad was alive (laughs).

Public Houses

Peter Boddy

Pateley High Street. I saw this picture on a calendar at Post Office a few years ago, so I bought the calendar and when I finished with it I had it framed cos it's a good picture of the High Street. It looks about 1900 or something like that. Might be before then.

It's got the step there, for mounting horses.

Mmm, I remember them steps.

They're gone now. The street's cobbled in the picture. They've put tarmac over them now.

Yeah, I don't like those cobbles, I'm glad they haven't got those now. It'd be bad walking on those I always think.

A lot of public houses closed now. There's the King's Arms closed. The Crown's still there. Other side of the street a bit higher up there were The Talbot and the... what was it... another one that was next door to it, then there was the Cross Keys up Church Street. The building's there, but it tin't a pub now.

Connie Bickerdike

What was it like in The Talbot?

Lovely. Well, we've stayed at the Knox Manor, which was before you got into Pateley. We've stayed at The Sportsman's. But at The Talbot we stayed for years and years, because that was a family owned place and we became friends.

What made it so special?

The size of it. Wonderful food. And such lovely people. And it was so clean. We went so many years that when we went there was always a bottle of wine on our table for a start.

Living in Towns

Peter Boddy

There used t' be railway come down to Harrogate. It were a nice run to Harrogate on railway.

When did the railway stop?

It finished about sixty, 1960, sixty four, something like that. And Council bought the land and built these houses.

And now there's buses into Harrogate.

I've been on t' bus into town. Used t' be a full one. Used t' be standing sometimes when you got to Harrogate. They say there in't many goes on it now. I don't know. Cos a lot has cars now, don't they.

John Rayner

I lost my wife six years ago. She were diabetic and blind and all sorts of disabled, so she died, but we've two right nice girls come and help us in house, yeah, from Pateley, aye.

People look after each other in a small community like this.

Yes.

You've never lived in a town?

No, I've been here all the time. I only have two girls in the house. Well, one comes and coooks for us and t' other comes and cleans up and does garden. Nowt posh, you know (laughs). I have same furniture as me granddad had. Table and corner cupboard and sideboard and all that. It's all same, do y' see? It's all same.

Connie Bickerdike

What was it like for a girl from the small village of Middlesmoor, ten years old, moving to a place like Bradford?
Terrible. Horrible. Horrible.

But I was happy at school. I went straight into Grange Girls' High school, which was in Great Houghton in Bradford. I was happy at school, but when we first got there, we moved into a little house in a row, and the street was a steep road, and as you sat on the outside toilet you looked out onto a mill chimney. It was frightening. You know, we'd never seen anything as big as... I can remember sitting on the outside toilet and there was this... but then we moved into a better house there. We were quite happy. But my brother Joe... my mother took him to school and by the time she'd got home, he was there first. He was the worst one for settling. That was my younger brother. My elder brother, he was laid back from the beginning I think (laughs).
Was the house in Bradford different from the one in Middlesmoor?
Oh yes, again... Bigger, and electric, and... Yes. It was very, very different.

Peter Boddy

Aye, I shouldn't like living in town, really. All houses are same and some of them say they don't know their next-door neighbour somehow.

Dinah Lee

You were young when you left Stean.
I was nine. It was just before the war when things were rock bottom. Prices of everything were rock bottom and that was when we

left and I went to live in Middlesmoor which was like an adventure for me, going into the town (laughs) because I had children to play with. There was a shop in the village. You know, it was a completely different life even though it was less than a mile away.

Houses

Connie Bickerdike

I can remember the smell of the farmhouse that we went into. There were always dogs. I don't think there were many cats about. There were always dogs in there, and of course when any sheep came to grief, we helped feed the lambs indoors near the fire. Yeah. Anybody could go in there. It didn't matter if you went in the front door or the back door. Everybody just... It was a thoroughfare. I don't know how Mrs Lee coped, I really don't. But to us, of course, she was always an old lady. She must've been an old lady because she worked so hard. I mean she had... Reg, Richard, Atkin, Norman, Mary, Lizzie... she had eight children and a farm. How she coped I can't just imagine. But as I say to us little ones she was always an old lady.

What was it like in the house with all that going on around?

I think only tidy on a Saturday! (Laughs) Because she had a huge table which was covered with oil skin, and there was always something on it, and Mr Lee always sat in his same chair.

What was the decoration of the room like?

(Laughs) Pretty grim I should think! That didn't interest us as little ones. We weren't interested. And of course everywhere were the home made rugs that were made from rags. That was one of the hobbies, rug making.

Busy woman!

Oh! Terribly. Terribly busy. No bathroom. I often think how on earth did people manage without a bathroom? Cos it was all this bathing in front of the fire.

No privacy?

Well, no. Because, with myself and two brothers, it was always Friday night, and of course they brought water at the side of the fire and had time to build up until it was really hot. No. I often saw the Lee boys stripped to the waist, washing at the sink.

Gladys Blakeson

Me grandmother brought me up because me mother had me before she married. I've a right tale! (Laughs) And she, me mother, worked at The Yorke Arms at Ramsgill. And when I was born the owners of The Yorke Arms were going to move away to Leeds because they bought the City Variety at Leeds.

Me grandmother said, 'You can go with them and I'll bring her up but you must send some money to keep her.' So me grandmother brought me up. But I allus had a mother, you see. When Grandma died, she was there, but she didn't die until I got engaged to Horace. She knew we were going to live there, same house you see.

Where was the house?

Lofthouse. Near the chapel. You know where the chapel is in Lofthouse as if you're going up over to Masham? Top of the village there's the chapel. And you went through there – there's a little sort opening between the back of them houses and the beginning of these houses – and you went to the end and we lived in the end one.

Dinah Lee

I can remember the old pantry and it had stone slabs. There were all these stone slabs round it because I remember the milk and things always used to be kept in there. What did I do once...? I went and stood on something and spilt a bottle of milk (laughs). I can remember getting into trouble from my step-brother. I don't know what I'd been doing, but I always remember getting into trouble cos I'd spilt all this milk.

Gladys Blakeson

That picture is the cottage that we moved out of to go into this one, and me grandmother wouldn't go back. She says, 'Oh, I's not going back there. I'm stopping 'ere. This is the end house.' So that's it. That's where I was born in that house.

Why did you move from one house to the house next door?

Well, that house had no water in it. You'd t' carry your water from the trough. No 'lectric light. No nothing when I was a kid. We had a paraffin lamp. No running water in. There was a sink in window, and a fire side which had a boiler what you filled with water for washing up and bathing in a tin bath (laughs) in front of fire when I was that age. And then that's why we moved out because he'd put 'lectric in, running water in and all the lot in this next one. They'd already done this one you see cos this was empty, so me grandma says, 'I'm not moving back again, I'm happy where I am.' So he says, 'Alright'.

Around the Village

Gladys Blakeson

I can remember Miss Hey were only person with a car besides one family that 'ad one up the village. There were only two cars. And I remember that lady that lived up the village, me grandma used t' send me round to her every Christmas and, 'Tek this evergreen and tell her your granny sent it and wish her well.' And I used t' have t' go around. And they were the only people with a car. It was one of those little ones. And we used t' think they were right posh cos they had a car! (Laughs) Oh dear! It were funny. Yeah, really funny.

Connie Bickerdike

Another thing, you see, with the whole village being so friendly if there was a farmer killing a pig we could go and watch. And that's where I learnt all my parts of pig, and we had to stir the blood for the black pudding, and we were never considered to be in the way.

We weren't a nuisance. Same with the sheep shearing. We used to go and stand and watch the sheep being sheared, then we watched the sheep dipping where the sheep went through all the disinfectant to stop all the bugs.

Dinah Lee
Saturday at The Bell Festival was a lovely day because I knew everybody. You know people. And you know their links and you know where their families are.

John Rayner
It's very remote living up here?
No.
Do you see many people during the week?
Yes. Well, these girls come from Pateley t' help us in house. Somebody's always ringing up, aren't they. And we have these farm walks where people come.

Christine Harker
Did you ever feel a sense of isolation up here?
No. Some people can't understand how you can get motivated, but when you've got a diary with fittings in you're working towards getting ready for that. Times when I was very busy I would work till two o'clock in a morning, you know, cos they were ready for something the next day or the day after.
You say you're trying to retire.
(Laughs) Yes!
What will you fill your time with when you retire?
Well there's all sorts of things that you hadn't been able to do cos you hadn't had time when you were self-employed. I've joined the Embroiderer's Guild and there's various programmes you can take part in if you can afford to do them.

green top :
milk delivered in glass milk bottles were sealed with foil lids,
the colour of which showed what sort of milk it contained.
Silver top was full fat pasteurised. Silver and red striped was
semi skimmed. Green top was farm fresh bottled.

*It was called fresh farm bottled in those days. We still got it – green
top – when we came down here.*

Rural Voice

Food
at Home

Photo: (Christine Harker) Lofthouse butchers

Food at Home

IN THE MEMORIES of the narrators, produce was often local, foraged or home grown – fruit, berries, rabbits, hens, geese, pigs, eggs, milk, butter. Food was kept cool in the pantry and meat hung from hooks in the ceiling at home. Pig killing took place on the farm where anyone could watch.

Home-Grown

Audrey Summersgill

We used to keep quite a few hens at the farm. We used to have some cockerels and the eggs used to go for hatching. A firm used to come round collecting them in those big boxes. Thirty dozens would there be. They used to take them to hatch. Well, we used to hatch a few ourselves. We used to eat the eggs. They were alright to eat until you started incubating them.

We used to eat the hens, what we called boiling fowls, like. Oh, they were tasty. We used to have a pressure cooker, well I still use pressure cookers. In them days you put it in the pressure cooker, like, it soon tenderised it rather, cos it took a bit of doing roasting them.

We used to kill two pigs up at Bewerley. During the war years we were allowed a pig a family. Somebody from Weatherhead's used to come. We used to have it on a big cratch and it were put on there and then you scalded it and scraped all the hair off with like these old fashioned candlesticks. Used to scrape all hair off with that.
Old fashioned candlesticks?
I remember this rusty looking thing we used to use. It looked like an old fashioned candlestick. I might not have been that at all. We used to have the copper on boiling there.

And then me uncle used to process it, like, to cut it up, and then he'd all the guts and such to deal with. You had the liver and bits for your tea. Pork doesn't taste like that nowadays! (Laughs) I mean, they were about twenty stone, these things. Big.

John Rayner

There were no turkeys when I were a kid. Every farm up this valley had a little flock of geese and if there were too many they gave a neighbour one. We always had a goose. There weren't any turkeys fifty, eighty years ago. Never heard of them. Now they rear them in thousands. America. They have them over there, don't they.

Goose. It were a tradition. Dickens' day. We had a little flock and they laid their eggs and hatched goslings, and if you wanted a new gander — they were male — you went away above Ramsgill for a new gander cos they were getting inbred. We carried it back in a sack. Raygill House up on top. You go to Ramsgill and turn straight up onto the moor bottom, don't you. Harkers. And we carried it back from moor bottom in a sack.

At Christmas you always killed a pig, didn't you. Every farmer had his pig ready for killing. Fat. Two. One killed before Christmas and one at Christmas. We shared it out with neighbours, pork, and you salted sides, and hams, didn't y'. Hung them up on them hoooks through there. I can remember, there used t' be a man come round killing pigs. He were an expert. By, it were a cruel business. But that's how it was.

Did you butcher the pigs yourselves?

Aye, out in one of buildings. And then you scrapped all its hair off. It had t' be right boiling water t' get its hair off. All bristly stuff. Scraped it all off. Pig killer just killed it, then he went to another farm, do you see? And me granddad, I can remember him hanging it up, opening its belly and then next day we cut it all up. We ate it for a week or two. And then pig's bladder, we used t' blow it up and play football with it. Yeah. There were no footballs when I were a kid.

Dinah Lee

To a certain extent you were self-supporting. Had our own milk, our own eggs and pig, you see, which they killed each year.

How would you have kept the meat?

In the dairy, in the cold pantry.

You'd hang it and salt it?

Yes. I can remember the hams and sides of bacon, we used to hang them from the ceiling (laughs).

My mother made butter, and kept hens, and loads of rabbits, and rabbit pies and things like that. The pig... there was always a pig on the go for pig killing, bacon and ham and things like that. Times have changed a great deal. We had a vegetable garden at the side of the house and they grew a lot of potatoes.

John Rayner

My dad once went to one t'owd Verities for his tea, and they gave 'im rabbit's head. They'd coooked a rabbit and they gave him t' head. Just head! And he'd t' pick brains out wi' his fork.

It was cooked?

Yeah! Coooked, aye, aye. They were that hard up, you see, and this rabbit were to share out wasn't it (laughs). You modern lasses, you don't know owt about things like that, do you! I remember you cracked the skull and picked brains out, aye!

I'd have to look at a rabbit's head a long time before I'd consider eating it. Would you boil it in a pot?

(Laughs) Aye, boil it, or in a pie probably. I don't know.

Eating

Connie Bickerdike

I can remember some of the things we had to eat. It would all be home made. Nobody bought anything. When I look back it must've been expense because we had to have our pudding before the meat, and the whole object would be you'd be full with your pudding so that you wouldn't need much meat. I always remember that. And my mum used to make the biggest steamed pudding, suet lined in a basin with fruit, and the lining of the basin was more than the fruit.

It was a bit heavy going. And another thing, we had to eat everything we were given. We hadn't to leave anything. You could have more if you wanted more, but you hadn't to leave anything on your plate.

Audrey Summersgill

What meals did you eat as a child?

Well, we always used to have a Sunday joint. Yorkshire pudding and the rest. And then you'd have it again on the Monday and gradually heat it up and it would end up as rissoles — mince it up and put veggies with it. I used to love rissoles; I haven't made any since. You just did 'em in the oven. We didn't deep fry them or anything.

What about bread and dripping? My dad used to love bread and dripping.

Oh. Yeah. I did, especially with that bit of browny bit at the bottom once it'd settled.

I don't think joints are so fatty these days.

No, they don't rear them like that now cos folks don't want fat. But you need a bit to cook it properly.

Connie Bickerdike

What about fresh milk?

We had an enamel can. I mean, you couldn't call it a jug. It was like a blue can with a lid on it and a handle and that's what we used to go down to the farm for, for our milk. We had fresh milk in the morning, fresh milk in the afternoon, and it must have been warm when we got it. No pasteurising or sterilising or homogenising. Just straight from the cow into this can and that was it until tomorrow morning when we had to nip down for more.

You wouldn't be able to keep it cool.

No. Oh no. Didn't do us any harm.

Did it have the cream on top?

Well, it hadn't had time to settle, but I mean that's what it used to do. My mum was very friendly with William's parents and we went on one occasion and Mary'd got the big bowl of cream, which was the top of all the milk. I don't know how old. And we used to churn that.

Whenever I went there to Woodale, Mary used to have me churn the milk to butter. And then of course I was taught how to use the butter pads and all the patterns that they used to make on the butter. And a lot of those sort of things went to the Pateley Show for prize winners and that.

And on one occasion I remember going with my mum, and Mary had made a load of scones and we had these scones with jam and all this lovely cream. Oooh they were lovely. And another thing she did was make scones with sour milk. Gorgeous. They were gorgeous. She didn't make fancy round ones. She rolled them out and they were all any sort of... They'd be hexagonal, or they'd be square, or... Never round ones, that was too fancy!

Can you remember the smell of the cream off the milk? Did it have a smell?

Yes. I can remember every smell.

What was it like?

...you're just... there.

Audrey Summersgill

I grow quite a few carrots in the garden and I only finished them end of February into March. I've quite a bit of soup in the freezer now; I'm making them into soup. And the beetroot, I finished that by about Christmas, so I make that into soup as well. I make a very delicious beetroot cake. It's really nice and moist. You put grated beetroot in, raw. And then I've got beetroot gingerbread as well. I think that's cooked beetroot.

Once we had a couple of plaques at Otley and I won the most points in the Young Farmers. 150th Otley Show, 18th May 1957.

Do you do a lot of shows?

I wouldn't say a lot of shows. Knaresborough I do now and Nidderdale. Those are the only ones I do now. Mainly vegetables, but I mean in Knaresborough you get some of these really professional ones. Behind you, those trophies on the shelf, they aren't all there, those are more or less for beetroot for Fellbeck Feast, if you've ever been to Fellbeck Feast, that's the Thursday after Pateley Show usually.

John Rayner

Me mother used t' make ginger beer. She put some sticks of ginger in or summat in a bowl, and did she boil it or not...? Have you seen them sticks of ginger?

Roots...

Roots, aye, roots. And they made ginger beer. Not mulled wine... Ginger beer, and Christmas cake.

And your mother made the Christmas cake?

Yeah. Oh yeah, proper. Iced it. Decorated it all with fancy stuff and those silver things. We always visited other farms during day, Boxing Day and later right up to New Year, you always went in and they always had a Christmas cake, hadn't they. B' time you got to end of January visiting all farms, it were going very dry, Christmas cake, cos they always saved it, for you visiting.

Did you know, they were trying to stop us drinking ginger beer some of Methodists? They said it were alcoholic. But it wouldn't be, would it? No. See, all farmers round about were Methodists, weren't they.

So no-one would be drinking mulled wine?

No. Well, you didn't know how to make it, did you. Me mum made nettle beer in summer. Right fizzy stuff.

Foraging

Connie Bickerdike

When things were in season we used to go down towards Stean, and when you've got over the bridge — there was the bridge from Middlesmoor to take you over the Nidd — and just to the right of there we always used to go picking hazelnuts. And another field not far from the vicarage we used to go and pick mushrooms. They were gorgeous. Oh, they were lovely things. But of course they were very seasonal... when the ground was very damp. And we had to go early morning cos they were there early morning, otherwise I think they used to disappear. Always in the same field.

What did you do with the hazel nuts?

Just eat them. Filberts, they call them now. Just used to eat them from the tree. Well, obviously collect some because they had some tough shells. They were lovely.

And then of course the other thing is the Stean plums. I knew Christine Harker's mum and dad. It's a long time ago, but I took my husband down to Stean and he met Mary and Fred Harker. Why I remember Fred Harker... he was such a good looking boy. He stood out from all the others. Fred Harker. He was a real good looking lad. We didn't mix much with people further down the valley. I think at the time he lived in Lofthouse.

Which was actually only about a mile away, or two, from you.

Oh yes.

Can you describe where the Stean plums were?

When you went into Stean, you went a long the little path or whatever it was, I don't suppose it was a road, you turned sharp right and the property is on your right. The Stean plums were in trees. I think there was more than one tree, opposite the properties, very very near the stream, cos the stream ran down the other side of the pathway.

What did you do with the Stean plums?

It was always jam. Talking to my brother, I said, 'Were they real damsons?' And Joe said that was always a mystery because they were only ever called Steam plums. But what lovely jam. They never actually said they were damsons. Damson fruit is a lovely fruit for jam. Just little dark plums.

Did you eat them straight off the tree?

No! Too sour.

Were you scrumping?

I don't think everybody and anybody went. I think it was only because you knew someone that lived there, 'Come when you like,' you know. It wasn't in a wild area like the hazel nuts were. And I think maybe whoever lived there at the time they would no doubt collect them and bring them up to Middlesmoor.

Cooking

Gladys Blakeson

How did you cook?
On t' fire! No electric. You had a paraffin lamp. You used to do your
kippers in front of fire. They had like a grate t' put her iron kettle on
to boil for your tea. Log and coal fire it was. And wood. And she used
t' get a big fork and put the kippers in between these... Lay it on these
slats of steel that was round fire and cook her kippers like that.

And there was a thing where you could hoook your pan on to it. She
had a big pan with a thing that went from one side t' other and she used
t' make stew in it and put in on the fire, cook it that way. Mmm.

And she used t' bake in oven on side. This side there was an oven,
that side was like a boiler, and middle was the fire. She used t' say,
'Go out and get some kindling. I'm gonna bake tomorrow, and I
want some wood. Some nice bits of wood t' go under oven. It needs
to be hot.' That's what you used t' have t' do.

Jack Haines

He were a funny old fella were Renton. He always knew when me
mother were baking at Scar. She always made him one of those little
brown loaves. He always knew which day it was to go to Scar. Him
and me dad started within a week of one another, when they were
first building Scar back in the twenties, well, nineteen hundreds or
whatever it was. Aye.

Connie Bickerdike

You talked about dying boiled eggs when you were younger.
That was always the parents. As children they were got ready for you.
Only two colours – pink or brown.

My mum used to boil tea, cos tea was loose, and she'd boil the tea
and it was dark brown, and the eggs having boiled in it for a while
until they were hard, a lovely dark brown.

The cochineal came from a little bottle. Beetle's blood, isn't it.

The old lady that lived in one of the cottages near the church, everything she made was pink (laughs). Her buns were pink, her cake was pink. I think maybe they called her The Pink Lady! It was a known fact in the village that everything... Miss Beech they called her... anything coming from Miss Beech was always pink.

to gowd (verb) :
to clip the sheep's tails before putting them to the tup.

We'll be gowding sheep tomorrow.

Rural Voice

Farming Life

Photo: (Anna Greenwood) Hay timing at Gouthwaite Farm, 2013

Farming Life

UPPER NIDDERDALE is a farming community. In the past there were also mills and rope makers along the River Nidd, but today it is predominantly home to sheep and store cows. The annual cycle of farming follows the seasons. Further down the valley the land is more fertile and supports dairy cows. Farms are owned or tenanted, and families have come in from other dales to work alongside existing families that have been in the Dale for generations.

Dinah Lee

They came as farmers. They lived somewhere just outside Reeth, but they came across to Nidderdale to farm. I remember my step-brother saying it took them three days to come over bringing all of their cattle. They brought their cattle, they brought everything with them, and it took them three days to come from Swaledale to Nidderdale bringing all their stock. They walked them. With their cattle and their goods and sheep. And they lived at a farmhouse called Thrope which is just up the Scar road.

What did they do at night?

I don't know whether they just lodged or whether they just curled up under a wall. I should have asked, but you see when you're younger you don't think of all these things.

John Rayner

In me granddad's day it were Yorke's estate. They owned it all from Bewerley right up to Stean and they had an agent just above Pateley and they were terrified of agent were the farmers. If they were doing things wrong they could kick 'em out of farm. Tenant farmers, you could not do what you liked. Every field had t' be mown, only work horses, had t' be no altering fences. Then they had gamekeepers, they were terrified of them. Me granddad used t' snare a few pheasants down in hedge, they used t' creep through hedge and get their necks caught.

And they were terrified if they got caught they could be sent to Australia for catching a deer or poaching. Good job it's altered, in't it! Aye.

Hay timing

John Rayner
In 1891 when Moses took over this farm, he bought a cutter, a machine for two horses, a mowing machine. First machine that came into Nidderdale. I have it at High Barn now, and in his diary it cost £7. A double horse machine. That did away with scything, didn't it. They thought it were marvellous, cos scything were hard work. They hired these gangs of Irishmen for scything.

Women all helped in them days out in fields, strewing about. Then it were to be heaped up into pikes, and then it were to lead in, fork in t' barn. There were little pikes, what you call cocks. They put them into that if it wasn't quite dry, little ones, shook them out next day and made them into bigger ones. Aye. It had to be dry else it went mouldy like.

How long did they stay up as pikes?

Well, they could stay a few weeks really, but bottom used t' go a bit rotten didn't it. We tied 'em down with ropes so as wind didn't blow 'em over. You twisted a hay rope, didn't you, between two rakes. You tied it over the top. Aye.

Did you make pikes?

Yeah. Up to '50s. We got our first tractor in 1948. Little Grey Fergie. Before that it were horses.

Jack Haines
We did some hay timing. Turning and strimming and rowing, all these jobs. With the rake. I think we enjoyed it. Just hand rakes, maybe a fork for a bit now and again. They had some beautiful horses, I can see them now... one called Owd Farmer. Beauties. Big. It was all done by hand and by horse.

Audrey Summersgill

We did have a lighter horse which used to do mowing and things like that. We used to turn the hay with that. One of the first jobs I did was raking clean. A big rake, used to go backwards and forward across the fields getting all the bits. Quite valuable you see, nice and clear.

Did you ride the horses?

I remember riding them when we were very little. They were so broad in the back, your leg were like this...! I remember going up for bracken, we used to maybe get a ride on the horse then, like.

The little ones we used to make were foot cocks. If it was just in bits of rows you got your rake and you sort of fetched a bit over like that and did it with your foot that way, and that was your little foot cock. You did that down the rows before it'd been too dry much. Then when it was getting nearly ready but not quite, and it was going to rain, you made jockeys. They were quite substantial really but you didn't trample them down or anything. You just made them with a fork and put the last bit on upside down so it shed the rain off a bit.

With the loose hay, we had a tractor and trailer we used to load up as well you see in the wagons, then we had sledges which me uncle used t' make with a runner at the front and wheels at the back. They were quite big, but you had to load them properly or else it slid off. And then you just back your horse up because there was a hook at the front and off you went to the barn with it.

Then we made pikes which were bigger ones. You used to stand on those and build them round yourself. You'd keep filling the middle up. They were like haystacks.

Then you had a pike bogie. It was just like a flat trailer with iron wheels on it and it was held down with a thing at the front, a pin through, and when you got to your pike you backed it up and if you had somebody with you, you pulled the front up a bit, generally with the horse, like, so far under the pike, then you got a big thick rope which was always used for tug of war in tug of war competitions (laughs)! Then you knotted it behind, then you had two levers on ratchets, two long levers like, and you pulled alternate you see, and you pulled it on. They didn't come apart. Then we got to pulling them with the tractor if they weren't too far away, fetching them as they were. They still stuck together. Farm man used t' come, 'Are we sniggling pikes today?' he used to say. Sniggling! Instead of snigging.

Stories

Jack Haines

There's all sorts of stories. Do you know John Beecroft? Well, Maurice Rispin, me, Willie Beecroft — that's his brother — and John were hay timing for old Myers and we were there turning. And owd Myers came down and was swinging his tap. We knew he were mad about something. We didn't get paid for anything, we were only kids, might have been ten or eleven. He comes down and he shouts, 'Middle man's missed a bit!' We looked at one another ... well, who's middle man of four? So, anyway, John, if he'd had a pint or two, like, said, 'Jack, come here! Middle man's missed a bit.' I said, 'Aye, I know, but who was it?' 'Buggered if I know,' he says (laughs). Owd Myers never paid us a penny, but my God we got well fed. We got really good food. And supper time every night, great big dishes of ham, fried ham. Tonnes of stuff. It's at Stripe. You come out of Wath over the bridge and go up, it's the first farm on the left.

Audrey Summersgill

We always called it The Farmstead, but now they call it Bewerley Home Farm which I suppose in a way is what it was really. Grandpa bought it in 1928 when the Yorke Estate was split up. But we lived in Cliff Cottage just up the field; there wasn't even a footpath to start with cos Mum had t' push this big pram up the grass. And then we made a single track, and then when it was sold we made another track so that it was enough for a car to go up.

It was always The Farmstead when we were there, I don't know why (laughs). It was a mixed farm. Mainly dairy cows. A few pigs and some sheep. A few poultry. About eighty acres. Then we used to have a bit more up under Guisecliff way. There was a few fields up there that we had as well.

I stayed on for a bit for the chappie who bought the farm, but he wasn't really farming. Then there was someone who lived up Top Wath Road near Wath and he asked my uncle if he would milk his cows for him while he went on holiday, you see. My uncle said perhaps Audrey would. So I ventured then into relief milking and anything else that was going really.

I can remember them milking by hand when I was little. There were two mistals ... there'd be ten cows either side and then a little one of six. So twenty six would be the most.

Did you have the suction machines?

Oh yes. It went into a bucket, called a unit, then when one cow was done you just emptied it and put on the next one. We never had the pipelines they have now. You had to carry it across the yard and then you put it into the side or the top which filtered any bits out that might be in, then it went down the surface cooler until they modernised and got one of these things that just sat on the top and there was cold water running through the tubes which cooled the milk that way, which is supposedly a bit better than these surface coolers.

What's a surface cooler?

It's all in and out, in and out, in and out like that. Lots of surface.

For quite a long time the milk went to a chappie with a dairy at Pateley Bridge and it was delivered locally.

Would that go to be pasteurised?

No. It was called Fresh Farm Bottled in those days. We still got it, green top, when we came down here.

I don't think they do it anymore.

They don't now. No.

John Rayner

There were no vets. If there were cow calving across that valley there, there used to be experts, bit like vets. Some farmers were better than others, wan't they, at calving a cow. Small hands. Could get inside. They hung a white sheet out of window over there if it were daylight and they wanted some help. Instead of a phone. They could see it, couldn't they.

Farming year

John Rayner

When spring comes in March we start calving these suckler cows and then when they go out to grass, calves are big enough to drink milk off cows. That's main time. And lambing time is in April. We don't lamb now (February) because weather's cold and there's no grass. So that's April, lambing time. We don't bring them in, they get behind walls. And if it's blizzards and wet nights it can be not so good. We can lose some.

We've had 'em scanned, that's a new thing now, isn't it. Scanning them for twins. And we had 'em scanned a fortnight ago and we know which of 'em has twins in now so we can give 'em a bit extra feed, can't we. And them with just one in them don't need as much. But them on moor, there's two or three thousand acres, we hadn't bothered with them, to scan, cos too big a job bringing them all to electric, like. But they mainly only have one on moor, just one lamb. Well, it's on poor grazing and they say after tupping time if they start off with two lambs inside them and they're on poor grazing, they reabsorb one of them so as they only have one. Cos they can't suck two on moor, they haven't enough milk for two, so they only want one.

When me granddad took over this farm in 1891 he hadn't much money and me grandma bought sheep on moor, and in 1890s there were some right hard winters and half of 'em died. Me granddad used t' say, 'Your money's dead on moor. All dead.' They never fed 'em in them days. Never entered their head t' feed sheep in them days. No. Hay were for cows, weren't it, inside. There were no cake t' buy.

William Verity

Going back to the early days, all the sheep were gathered down to the sheep pens at the beginning of September and all the lambs were taken off for spaining and the mothers put back on the moor.

On the 15 October, all sheep were gathered in again for dipping. That were compulsory, dipping, in those days. You had t' come down home to dip and usually an inspector came to watch you dip. And they had t' have a minute each. And, oh, it's a terrible long time is a minute. But we had one chap came once, he was a retired police man, and we were making it last trying to get minute and he says, 'Get it out! You're gonna drown it!' before minute were up.

Do their heads go under as well?

Yes. Oh yes. Two or three times. That was for scab. Dipped thousands of sheep over years. We use now an injection for it.

They're not dipped anymore?

Well, not if we can help it. We dip a few o' lambs. Then we use this injection now. Rather expensive but it's very hard work dipping sheep.

Bracken

Gamekeeper

A problem we had on the moors was the bracken. Going back before days of the little bales of hay and straw, the farmers used to cut the bracken for bedding. Now, that kept it under control. But when the little bale came along and they started baling straw it was good to deal with, good to handle, so they stopped cutting the bracken and the bracken exploded. And that came onto us to control the bracken. We used to roll it. There was a roller you put on the back of a tractor, back and forward, and you crushed it and the bracken bled. And eventually you could control it. Nothing eats it. It's a total waste. It's good for nothing.

Then along came a chemical and they devised a chemical to control the bracken and that's what happens today. They spray it, mostly by aircraft.

William Verity

Do you have bracken up on the moors? John has bracken and they used to use it to bed cows.

Oh, it's very good for bedding. And each farmer had a certain plot on the moor that he went and cut and dried and led home, but you see when they started being modern in eighties there with these agents, they had it all sprayed by helicopter you see to kill it all, so most of it were killed off on Stean, I think. John has some, I think he has some inside land with bracken, and it's very good to cut, even with a mower. He might still get some, John.

Audrey Summersgill

We used to collect bracken. We had a patch up in the wood that we could utilise. It made jolly good bedding. John Rayner used to bale it.

John Rayner

We started baling bracken and we used t' get a thousand bales a year off of moor bottom. It were all rocky, y' had t' be careful. It saves buying straw.

Do you do it now?

No, it's too rough on moor.

For the machines?

Yeah, aye.

Before that it would've been done by hand...

Yeah, mowing with scythes and then leading with horses onto carts and that. They ought t' have bedding for cattle inside and now we have t' buy straw and it's awful price. It's £80 a tonne coming from Ripon, and there's no pay at that.

Sheep

William Verity

'Hogs' are replacement female sheep. They become ewes the following year. 'Heft' is where they've been brought up they go back to exact same place. We say 'hoof', but I think proper word's 'heft'. We stopped after a while, we decided to do it all at once because it was damaging a lot of lambs all this gathering. So, what we did, we clipped hogs at same time as mothers and sheep. 'Spaining' (laughs). It's a word we use for taking them from their mothers. Their mothers go back to moor immediately. A lot's kept for replacement. And others sold around November time. Verity's sheep go right to the top and it's about four and a half miles from Stean to boundary. It was all open common but back in the eighties they had Sir Joseph Vickerson bought moor and he put a fence right round! Cos we were bothered with so many other sheep off other moors, particularly Ramsgill way, cos it were better ground you see for them. So that stopped them.

John Rayner

If them on moor lamb two, odd ones, we take one off for pet lambs cos you end up with right little bad'uns and yau goes thin. Half of them are on moor and half down in grass fields, and we're feeding them cos they've more twins in 'em.

How many sheep do you have?

About 500. On moor you've got to breed them on moor else they go away. Stop where they're born, don't they. Well, that's the idea. You've heard of it, haven't y'? 'Hefted'. Or 'hoofed' they call it. If we sell this farm to somebody, those sheep have to go to next owner because they belong on moor, they don't stray t' Greenhow or Stean or Middlesmoor because they belong farm. Not if they're born there. If you bought 'em, they'd go for miles.

Have you got your own mark on them?

Yeah. Moses Rayner. MR. On t' horn, you burn it in don't you. Each farm has their own flock, their own patch of moorland even though

there's no fence and they're supposed to stay where they're born.
And they do?
Yeah mainly, apart from stragglers. We go to Grassington for odd
ones, go over top. And to Greenhow we go for odd'uns, and we go
for odd'uns to Stean, like, but bulk of 'em stay where they're born.
How do you know where they've gone to?
Neighbours ring up. They know our mark. Every farm has his own
mark. We've been here that long, they know MR.
What kind of sheep do you farm?
Swaledales. Them wi' horns on. You've seen 'em, haven't y'?

Reminiscing

Audrey Summersgill
Did you have any duties when you were a child?
I always used to be helping where I could, and me mother used to
play pop with me carrying buckets of chopped turnips across the big
yard there to some animals that were tied up.
What was that expression – your mother used to play pop?
Well, it's not quite being cross with you, but getting that way (laughs).
Carrying buckets of turnips when quite small, really.

Connie Bickerdike
We used to go and stand and watch the sheep being sheared, then
we watched the sheep dipping where the sheep went through all the
disinfectant to stop all the bugs.
Who would do the sheep shearing?
The farmers themselves. Oh yes, they didn't employ people to come
in and do it. The farmers did it themselves.
By hand?
Yes. Oh, no electric gadgets, no.
*Because electricity wouldn't have come to Middlesmoor when you were there,
would it?*

No. No. I can remember the smell of the farmhouse we went into. When any sheep came to grief we helped feed the lambs indoors near the fire.

Dinah Lee

That's James in the photo. That was a pet lamb. Dear me! It was a bad winter and a lot of farmers were just losing their lambs. We ended up with this lamb. We kept it in the house in a box. James (laughs). In the end James got too big for his box. So there was a paddock at the top of the village where we had a shed, so James was put in this shed, and he was allowed out during the day on the grass and he had a chain... (laughing). There was one night we were in bed and I heard this noise of a chain rattling and James bleating outside like mad! He'd got loose and come home (laughing)! He'd come all the way down the village dragging his chain behind! I think my husband had to get up and take him back. He wasn't happy. Poor old James. He had to go to market eventually.

to lamp (verb) :
hunt at night using lamps, in this case for foxes.

We lamp the fox at night. A lamp on top of the vehicle with a handle inside. One person is driving the vehicle and another person is doing the lamp. You find the fox, and if it's safe you dispatch them with a high powered rifle, and you spend a lot of time on that, especially at night.

Rural Voice

Grouse Moors

Photo: *The duty of loading*

Grouse Moors

MOORLANDS ARE owned by landowners. Some areas are farmed by farmers, and others looked after by gamekeepers. Farmers manage their sheep to maintain the health of the land, and gamekeepers manage the land to raise healthy flocks of game birds. These vast areas of moorland are overseen by men and women living in the remotest parts of the Dale.

Sheep on Moors

Christine Harker

Each farm is entitled to so many sheep gaits, and a gait is G-A-I-T. It entitles a sheep and its followers on to the moor. So, say you have sixty sheep gaits, it means you could have sixty sheep – plus a hundred and twenty lambs if they all had two lambs each – that year. And then the lambs are sold off and it starts all over again. Some farms aren't farmed anymore and the sheep gaits have been sold off to another farm.

The sheep stay because they're hefted?

That's right. I mean, they'll keep so many of the lambs and sell so many of their older sheep to keep the flock renewed all the time. The sheep spend most of the time on the moor, but when they get nearer lambing they'll bring them in.

William Verity

There's only three farmers now have sheep on the moor and now they're gathered in by dog and on quad bike. It used to be just walking and dogs. A lot of walking, like. My son has a very good dog. If they hadn't quad bikes they couldn't manage. But what they do now, they do it in three, four days, gradually, which is far better for sheep. We used to set off very early in the morning, say 8 o'clock, and it'd get to 4 o'clock in afternoon by time you got sorted out. They all had different areas, and they worked them all together to bring 'em

Photo: (Paul Harris) Sheep gathering on Stean Moor, 2017

down as one packet. I used to dread them days, chaps falling out and dogs fighting. A lot of lambs got 'broke down' we call it, damaged their legs. I think in them days they didn't get the food they get now and they were very easily broken, the bones in their legs. You can have as many as ten damaged, and if it's their back leg they never come right.

Back in them days there were a massive amount of sheep. Them sheep belonging other moors, could've been three or four hundred of them on as well, from Ramsgill and Grassington and Middlesmoor. We used to get more sheep from other moors when we gathered than there is on now all together, till we got it fenced.

Now, three of them go with quad bikes and dogs. Bring them to pens just the same, but they do it in four lots. It does it nicely now. It was terrible back in them days, I used to dread gathering. In our case, there's a cripple hole straight out of pen into our field, but rest of them walked them home.

Stean Moor is an outstanding moor. Gouthwaite Moor, John's, is all heather. Stean Moor will suck a half bred lamb, that's a crossbred lamb, but John's wouldn't. Different all together. As you come further up from Heathfield right up Ramsgill, Ramsgill's very similar to Heathfield. And then you get onto Stean there's a lot of heather and then a big patch of 'white ground'. It's a kind of benty grass. And then you get over onto Middlesmoor side – Steven Ramsden's – and it's similar ground to Stean is theirs. About a third I would say... a third of it's heather. Joining Ramsgill, as you get further north it runs out a bit

In the Eighties the government scheme came out with grants for landlords to do gripping on the moors. Stean Moor owners applied for a grant and us farmers were against it. We have these annual meetings and we were really against it because we didn't believe in it. Anyway it went ahead, didn't it.

What's gripping?

Gripping, well, it's taking a gully out like a dyke about two foot wide by two foot deep. It turns sod right over and leaves this big channel. Terrible it were. We were against it like, cos we'd seen it on other moors. We owned our own sheep rights – that's what landlord said – but we didn't own the sods. And that's what they were interfering with, wasn't it, turning it over.

A great big machine cutting out a great big trench which we thought could be dangerous even for sheep – I mean, young lambs. Awful size it were. If little grouse dropped in, they'd never get out and if they followed down they'd come at water and drown, little places where water used t' stand. A lot of them, a little young lamb would have a job too. They don't go back t' moor till they're quite strong, but I think a new born lamb wouldn't have got out if it dropped in.

A large area of the moor was gripped, and when the first heavy rain or a thunderstorm came water came off the moor so fast, damaging our small streams around Stean. Oh, if it came a thunder storm, within half an hour water coming down. And it did a lot of damage t' banking sides and things like that cos it were coming off too fast, you see. Moorland kind of holds the water, doesn't it, moss and peat, and it gradually runs away.

This went on for quite a few years and when the same problem was happening in other areas a new scheme came out where you could get a grant to have them all filled in (laughs). Ah, there were a rumpus on up Swaledale and them valleys, you know. Terrible, I think. Same thing were happening.

Stean Moor applied for a grant and was successful and over the next two years at a considerable cost they were filled in. I did not know what to think about it at the time, but it has proved a real success. It has. We were frightened there could be sheep drowned, but do you know, it's been alright. Better for quad bikes. It's worked well. Oh, it cost hundreds of thousands. Luckily Stean's owned by Lord Vesty and you had to stand so much but you got it back so we didn't lose out much in end. It were mainly paid for by grant.

Game Birds and Shoots

Gamekeeper

What is a typical gamekeeper's day?
Taking the spring of the year... if it was dry enough you'd get on with your burning. That's your number one job — get on with as much burning as you can. And then, if you're on with predator control, you have to check those cage traps twice a day to see that everything was okay and nothing was taking any harm. Check your stoat traps, your rat traps. Continuously check them.

Then we lamp the fox at night. A lamp on top of the vehicle with a handle inside. One person is driving the vehicle and another person is doing the lamp. You find the fox, and if it's safe you dispatch them with a high powered rifle, and you spend a lot of time on that, especially at night.

Day and night. You're always on the outlook for the poacher and the thieves. We've had some from Bishop Auckland in Durham.

Mostly from West Yorkshire. The poacher was after the animals and the birds. And thieves, mostly pinching stone.

It was continuous. Then, during the summer if it was very very dry you had to fire watch. You had to keep an eye that there was no summer fires. Cos that's deadly, a summer fire. It doesn't only affect the wildlife, but it can burn the ground out as well, kill all the plants off once it gets into the peat.

How do you manage the burning so that it doesn't burn the ground out?

By beating, and by not burning it when it's too dry. Once it starts getting too dry, you stop it. You're asking for trouble if you continue.

And the burning season stops April the fifteenth?

That's right. Everything's starting to nest then. But down here these lower moors we finish thirty first of March because things here are much earlier than say at Reeth and Tan Hill. Much earlier.

Shooting starts on twelfth of August, that's the grouse, and it finishes on the first of February. All the shooting seasons finish on the first of February. Grouse comes from the twelfth of August to the tenth of December. Partridges, they start on the first of September. And pheasants start on the first of October and they run until the first of February.

It's great excitement, the twelfth of August, the grouse shooting season. It's the only country in the world that do it; the only country

Photo: (Gladys Blakeson) Shooting party.

in the world that's got red grouse. It's a very exciting day. And the grouse runs from the twelfth of August to the tenth of December.

After that you don't shoot grouse?

It's unlawful. They're starting to pair up then.

When people come to help with the beating, where do they come from?

There's a lot people that love coming beating. They come for the exercise and they enjoy it. And once you've got that list you stick to your list and you get them every year.

There's two sorts of beating, aren't there. There's beating of the fires, and there's this beating that we're talking about which is beating of the birds.

That's right. With the flags. You had people that could help you with both.

Can you tell me what a beater's job would be with a flag?

It all depends where the wind is. You try to take out what we call a 'drive' with the wind so the beaters would line right out around here, with what we call flankers on each side, three or four on each side. There's a line of shooting butts there and they flag the grouse towards the butts. The beaters are the ones who are actually moving, and they're beating their flags to get the grouse to move.

They're closing the grouse in.

That's right.

What colour flags?

Could be red or white.

And the beaters are coming in with their flags...

That's right, waving their flags to get the birds to rise.

And how do the beaters not get shot?

Safety comes into it. We've got a horn. Probably when you're one hundred and fifty yards from the butts. Once that horn's blown, no more shooting in front. If anybody shot in front after that they're sent home immediately. You only then turn round and shoot behind the butts. If anybody did shoot in front after the horn, they're in trouble, and rightly so. And then footpaths, you've got to watch footpaths as well. You've got to think of the public, and you set your flank out so that when anybody appears on the footpath the flag goes up and shooting stops. You can ask the people to stay, and some of them do, they'll say 'OK, we'll wait till your drive gets through.' If they don't want to stay, you mustn't hold them, you must let them through. Up goes the red flag, shooting stops, until the people pass and then the flag comes down again. You've got to do it. People's safety comes first. First. Absolutely first.

Do most of the beaters come from around this area?

Yes. But some of them come from... some come forty miles beating. They love it, they enjoy coming up. They enjoy the exercise, they love the company, and it's a great atmosphere. You all get on well together, you have a bit of craic, you pull legs (laughs).

Most of the moors round here, they lunch in the lunch hut, and the lunch is brought out to the hut and they have it there, and there's also in many cases a hut for the beaters to sit in and they go and have their lunch in there.

Are the birds migratory?

The lapwing migrate. The curlew migrate. The grouse will stay, unless you get a very severe snow storm, and they do move then. We had some in the '78–'79 winter up here. A friend of mine rung me up at lunch time one day, he said, 'I've seen a pack of grouse hit the electric wires.' I think it was thirteen hen grouse it killed. And they were from Reeth, so they'd come a long way. They were hunting for food. All the moors were snowed under and iced over. That was a bad winter.

John Rayner

Twenty fourth of April in 1981, you wouldn't hardly be born, biggest blizzard ever buried all our lambs and it brought Harrogate Flower Show tents down. Twenty fourth of April. Can you believe it? The grouse were nesting on moor. They were sat on their nests, on eggs, and got buried. They made a tunnel out. Some laid again, some lost 'em. They didn't expect that, did they? I know it killed a lot of blackbird nests in hedges. Snow settled down deep onto hedges and smothered them.

William Verity

There have been big improvements over the last few years with considerable amounts of grouse, with a record number shot in 2014 and a very similar number in 2015. I think there were about four hundred and fifty brace first day a year or two ago, and yet all rest of moors round have had very low numbers.

Is that down to the gamekeepers?

I suppose partly, but whether they'll come again, I don't know. John Rayner says it won't last, you're sure to get a bad year.

Gamekeeper

I've met some wonderful people. I met Bing Crosby. His wife came with him, Kathleen. Bing was marvellous company (laughs). When you finished a day's shooting you were walking back to the vehicles, if you come up near him and you hummed one of his songs, he would set off! Marvellous.

I once was asked to go down to Staffordshire to look after the late Lord Litchfield and he had somebody accompany him. I wasn't told who it was until that morning and it was Princess Margret, his cousin, and I looked after them for the day, and it was a fantastic day. It really was a very funny day. A very happy day was that.

Do you still get onto the moors now?

Yes, still go out. And enjoy it. And no responsibility! (Laughs) Can just go out and enjoy it.

(His wife): You've got your memories, that's the main.

Absolutely. Absolutely.

spiced pig (noun) :
a sweet made out of sugar in the shape of a pig.

And Father Christmas, when we were kids, all we got was a stocking with an orange in and a spiced pig. Have you seen a spiced pig? They've a little woolly tale on 'em. It were all sugar. Like a sugar mouse. They still mek 'em don't they. Aye, well it were a sugar pig. That's all we got.

Rural Voice

Annual Events

Procession 1903

Photo: (Dinah Lee) The annual Middlesmoor Bell Festival, 1903.
From A Stone's Throw From Heaven

Annual Events

CELEBRATIONS AND PARTIES are ways of sharing stories and honouring events in the calendar. Alongside the well-known celebrations of Christmas and Easter are events that take place according to the moorlands' cycle of shooting. Other traditional events take place that are particular to the Dale itself and that have been enjoyed for generations. We start in June with memories of the Bell Festival, which celebrated its 150th anniversary in 2018. It marks the donation of a peel of six bells to Middlesmoor church in 1868 and it is a festival of great importance in the Upper Dale and one of the highlights of the year.

Bell Festival — June

Connie Bickerdike
Then there was Bell Festival which was a great festive few days in Middlesmoor. Dinah, a wonderful friend still living up in Pateley Bridge, she was in charge of the Bell Festival for years. Of course, she was a teacher. And then at the Bell Festival it was all devoted to the children of the village and we had to do a wild flower floral arrangement and there was a prize for the winner. But to go and collect the flowers was sheer joy because there was such a variety of flowers, and of course we didn't have fancy vases, they were all done in a jam jar. We found the flowers all around the village, down in How Stean Gorge, there were blue bells, red campions...
Did you do the arrangement yourself?
Oh yes! No cheating.

Dinah Lee
I've always been involved with church and the Bell Festival. Until recently I organised it for years and years, which I felt quite pleased about because it was on the point of dying out. It used to be on a Thursday. The children had the day off, but a lot of people were at work and

the numbers dropped and dropped. I remember there used to be only about thirty in church at one count and it was really quite difficult, so we had a little discussion and we decided to change it to a Saturday and it took off. People weren't at work, they were free to go, you got more helpers, and over the years it's really grown from something that was on the point of dying out to something that I'm sure now will carry on.

August 12th

Connie Bickerdike

From Bell Festival we came to August the twelfth, a great celebration in the village. Everybody was involved. There were the beaters and the pony boys, and as the younger ones we had to go and open the gates for the gentry all coming back from the moors on horses. You opened the gate when you could see... 'Ooh, they're coming! They're coming!' And when they got to the open gate, they threw silver thre'penny bits on the floor. Sometimes you might get a sixpence. We never opened a gate with maybe more than two or three of us, so whatever you picked up it was divided equally.

Who were the pony boys?

Anybody. Boys from the village or young men. They would look after the horse... got it ready for the start of the hunt, and then care for them and feed them and take them back home because they were horses that belonged to the local farmers. I remember one jolly chap that used to come, a big fat chap, and of course we remember him. He was always smiling.

Pateley Show — September

John Rayner

That's Moses, and his wife Harriet looking out of the door. And there's this cow that won this cup at Pateley Show. Same cow. That cow. Prize cow. What does it say on it? It says: Nidderdale Agricultural Show 1902. Aye, that's it. President's prize for Best Beast. Aye, that cow there. Is it silver?

Photo: (John Rayner) Moses Rayner's prize winning shorthorn cow, Gouthwaite Farm

Connie Bickerdike

Mr Lee always won the prizes for his hens and he specialised in Bantams. And when there was a show coming, and he was fanatical, he had these chickens on the table, on the oil cloth where everybody had their meal, and he'd be pruning them and shaping them, and getting them ready for Pateley Show.

November

Connie Bickerdike

Now we're into November. All the village used to gather for the bonfire. We always had jacket potatoes done in the fire. That was a treat. No big bangs. We were only allowed sparklers. That was the only firework we knew. I suppose the men of the village got the fire ready, always on November the fifth. It was on a field just walking along past Dovener House. You would have seen it from Gouthwaite Hall.

November the eleventh, all the school were taken out to the cenotaph, Remembrance, November the eleventh. Yeah. I don't think we had music... we didn't have music around the cenotaph cos it was too... I mean you really got the blow of the valley right up against you, didn't you. Yeah.

December

John Rayner

Father Christmas when we were kids, all we got was a stocking with an orange in and a spiced pig with a little woolly tail on – it were all sugar. A joiner at Ramsgill once made me a little wheel barrow and I used t' wheel my sisters about in it and we were on in dyke and I tipped them off into water! (Laughs)

What about Christmas presents?

There were no wrapping paper. I can't remember getting a present from under the tree. It's changed. We got this one stocking, it were hung at bottom of bed and that were it, and where it came from we didn't know. Kids are spoilt now. Computers and text things and all sorts. Aye. If one wants it, t' other wants it, don't he.

And when you got to be teenagers you played games. Black Magic, have y'heard of that? Y'had a poker and had t' guess what was coming next, and secret was you touched something black before answer was. It were a complicated thing. Then we used t' play Postman's Knock. All girls used t' put their names in a hat, teenage girls, and then you put your hand in, drew one out, then you went into passage there for kisses and that and if you got a good looking one you were well away! You didn't come out so quickly (laughs). Me mum and dad used to be sat through there when we were all teenagers, about fifteen of us in here, and we were always going out playing Postman's Knock and they could hear us and me mother put clock on two hours. She were that fed up she shoved it on from ten to midnight and it were time to go home. Cos teenagers go a bit crackers in a group.

Did you send Christmas Cards?

No, we delivered them b' hand round about. When did post first start up here? Me dad and me mum never got any Christmas Cards, not like we do. It's come in later, hasn't it. And there were no phones. We got phone in about 1950 and afore that you wrote letters. There weren't even any cards. Sometimes if people were on holiday you got a postcard, but there were no Christmas Cards when I were a kid, and now there's thousands. I don't remember us having Christmas Cards, or any luxuries at all. It were war time.

Lofthouse and Middlesmoor had a band, brass band, came round every farm at Christmas playing carols. You looked through windows and they were out there.

How many farms would there be around here?

There's two at next farm. They're private houses now. Raygill House, two. One there, two up there, and a few on Heathfield and a few in Wath. Maybe ten within striking distance, two or three miles like. There were no good singers — not like these choirs you see on telly.

Just people singing.

Yeah — carols.

Can you remember any of the carols you used to sing?

Well, While Shepherds Watched and all them. Not pop songs cos telly's full of pop songs now — White Christmas, Do They Know It's Christmas and all them. They came afterwards. Seventies.

White Christmas.

That's the best one. First one, weren't it. On a film it wur.

Do you still have carol singers coming today?

No. Given up. Young Farmers used to come round from further down. They've given up.

When would that have stopped?

They were coming up to 20 years ago when my wife Mary were about, and we invited them in and gave them a drink, and they were collecting mainly for charity, or club. Not for theirselves. Kids now go carol singing round the streets for their own money, if their hard up. It isn't meant for that, is it (laughs). No.

Easter

Connie Bickerdike

Easter Monday, the children of the village all had hard boiled eggs which we rolled down Church Bank and the winner was the one that got down without being cracked or smashed. But it didn't matter at the end of it whether yours were cracked or smashed, we all ate the eggs.

May

Connie Bickerdike

For the Maypole, the girls, we all used to have to have the same dresses, the same material. And Miss Ridley used to choose the material, which had to be green and yellow, and then the parents made the dresses. But Miss Ridley had the choice of material and colours. Oh it was ... bells, joy... There's nothing like it today. Nothing like it.

Dinah Lee

Maypole Dancing... I remember! Poor Brian! (Laughs) My youngest was about five when we were short of people to do the Maypole (laughing). So he had to take part, but he couldn't do the hop skip, so he ran! They sort of do a skip as they do it, but Brian had to do a run to keep up. And you had this old wind up gramophone over in the field for them to dance to. You know how it runs down, it would go nicely away, and then all of a sudden it would go *uuuuurrrrr* and I used to have to run and wind it up (laughter)! Oh dear! It was all good fun.

yau (noun) :
local pronunciation of 'ewe', a female sheep.

And me dad started teking Sunday school in afternoon, and one of pupils said he didn't hear much about Jesus, but he heard plenty about yaus and tups!

Rural Voice

On a
Sunday

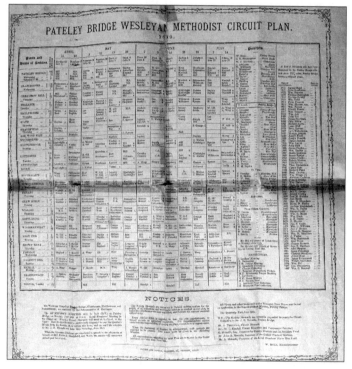

Photo: (Ann Smith) Pateley Bridge Wesleyan Methodist circuit plan 1889

On a Sunday

SUNDAY WAS a day of rest for man, woman and beast. Churches and chapels drew the community together to worship and talk about the week. First there were the Catholics, then the Anglicans, and then John Wesley brought Methodists to the Dale. In this less regulated form of worship local people become preachers and Sunday school teachers. Work and leisure took on a different form on a Sunday to the other six days of the week.

Chapels

John Rayner

There were eighteen chapels in Nidderdale as far as Summerbridge... New Houses, way b' Scar, Bouthwaite, Wath, Pateley, and then you spread out t' West End, din't y', Fellbeck, and Kettlesing way down b' Birstwith. There were eighteen. And now there's Wath, Pateley, Summerbridge and Darley.

A lot have been converted into houses.

Aye, all of them, mainly. The chapel at Wath has five sides.

Who built it?

Local folk. Those owd Rayners were one of them. Sort of religious, aye.

Peter Boddy

And I know you through the Pateley Bridge Methodist church, that's where we met. Did you go to Methodist churches when you were younger?

I've been to Pateley chapel, Greenhow chapel, and I've been to the church, but I wouldn't say I were regular like I am now. When we came t' Pateley, when we were at Foster Beck, me mother started going to Heathfield chapel, that's up the hill over the bridge and turn left. When we were about five or six we went there. When that closed, went to Wath, and then we came t' Pateley. Me grandfather was a local preacher for forty years round here, William Boddy. Methodist.

Sam Hesselden

Pateley Methodists, they've had a lot of alterations done at their church. They've spent many many many thousands. They've redone it and it's beautiful. Well, it took 'em six months and while they were having theirs refurbished, a massive project, while they were doing that they asked Wilsill if we would let 'em come t' join, and we said 'Yes', and there were forty of them come. We could seat eighty. And they came every week to Wilsill. They gave us a fair boost. It lifted it up. But now you see time come when their own opened again and it were a big opening. They come to us every so often but there in't a lot. We want some new comers. Y' can't say t' someone. They have t' come of their own free will. We've done our best. How long it'll last we don't know.

We always go there regularly, every week we go t' service. It's just how things are. We feel alright and happy and content. It's only a little place, there's only a handful of us now, they've got less wi' people dying and going on. We don't seem to be getting anybody back in their places. We could do with some more members, but I don't know where they'd come from. Things have changed. You'd hardly believe it. There used t' be two services every Sunday. One in afternoon and one in evening, half past six, well now there's only one in a morning, eleven o'clock while twelve. One a week. How long that'll last I don't know cos members are going down. We can see it coming.

William Verity

Matthew Verity married a girl out of Ramsgill called Elizabeth Nicholson. He had five sons and I think he took a family of four with him to America, and one of them was called Jonathan, one of Matthew's sons, and he was an evangelist, a bit like Billy Graham, religious man, evangelist chap. Jonathan travelled all over world and he came into Europe in 1909 and came to Pateley Bridge and he opened new chapel at Pateley, as you go out top of street, Methodist chapel, and preached there.

Sam Hesselden

Has church been a big part of your life?

Oh, yes it has. Me mam were a staunch Anglican. I went to Sunday school, Methodists, from being six years old, and then when I were sixteen years of age they presented me wi' a bible. It's a lovely bible, King James' version and it's written in it when it wur, nineteen forty something, and it's too small a writing for me now. I have another one, but it's a Good News that. I stopped there when I wur sixteen and we used t' go regularly. Me brother used t' go with me and that was at Methodists cos we liked that form of service better than Anglican, although we're joining together more than ever. We go there and they come to us.

I've been lucky. I've been Steward down at chapel 'ere, at Wilsill. Methodists call them Stewards. George Bradley were Steward for

Photo:
(Anna Greenwood)
Wath Chapel carol
service 2016

thurty six years and I took it over from him when he were poorly. He lived while he was ninety seven did George Bradley. He were Methodist and he lost his wife. He looked after his wife for more than twenty years. He wur a good man.

My son, Stephen, he did all exams and he's a local preacher. Methodists call it a local preacher. He's been a local preacher for, oh, syne he were about nineteen year old. He's very very good.

John Rayner

Me grandfather, Moses, went three times a day to Wath chapel, on a Sunday. In a morning they went t' service, walked. In afternoon, there were Sunday school, and then they went for another service at night. Farmers didn't work on a Sunday in them days. Horses wanted a rest. Nidderdale were all Methodists, all these chapels... they went t' chapel. Aye. It's all died out now, you see. There's different religions. Catholics and Protestants and Jehovas Witnesses. Nobody goes now. They clear off in cars. Somebody's lent me a boook about all different religions and funerals and all that. And they're on about eternal life, aren't they, these preachers. It says half of folk in England are bored on a wet Sunday afternoon... so what good's eternal life to them? They're bored in one afternoon!

Connie Bickerdike

And Mr Million was the minister at Middlesmoor then?
Yes, Mr Million.
Did he take the services?
Yes. My eldest brother was in the choir and one Sunday he came home and I can remember my mum said 'Who was at church this morning, then?' He said, 'A million and one,' because he was the only one there! (Laughs) He was the only one there, yes.

There were the very regular ones that went because we, as children, didn't go to many of the services in church because we always had to go to Sunday school. And that was another happy memory of Sunday school, which was down in the vicarage where Mr Million lived.

That's a big house.

Oh, a lovely house. When we went in there into the kitchen with Mrs Million... I can remember that Sunday school was upstairs. And there again we had to learn hymns and the stories. It was lovely, and we enjoyed it.

Which hymns?

Most of the most popular ones. And even now if I watch Songs of Praise I do it purely to see if they're still singing the hymns that I learnt.

Sam Hesselden

We're part of *Church In The Dale*. They meet at Show Ground especially on Show Day, Nidderdale Agricultural Show, and they have a tent there and we mix there. There's a Catholic church opposite, going t' Pateley on your right, before y' get int' Pateley. And then there's St Cuthbert's at top of School Hill in Pateley, and St Michaels here (Wilsill) and they have a church, Anglican, at Greenhow, but I don't know if they meet once a month or once every two months, it's only steady. And they have one at Ramsgill... that's about same... Anglican. There used t' be a Methodist at Fellbeck, that closed, it's a house now.

I don't know what outlook'll be. It'll have t' alter if it's gonna last any much longer.

Work

Audrey Summersgill

Well it's funny really, Mum came to Glasshouses church and Dad went t' Pateley (laughs) and Uncle Harry went to Pateley. But Dad was a local preacher as well.

Would that have been Methodist?

Yes.

So he was busy on a Sunday.

He would have to dash off to his appointments although generally they were in the afternoon, like. He'd probably one or two evening ones as well.

Did he ever work on a Sunday?

They never used to hay make. There were ructions one time – it was a day this hay was ready and it was a really bad forecast. Anyway, it was a Sunday. Dad didn't help, it was me uncle and myself and I think we had a farm man in those days. We got this hay up on a Sunday (laughs). I said, 'Well, I'm sure the Lord wouldn't mind us giving our animals a bit of decent hay instead of a load of rubbish!'

I mean, obviously we had t' milk the cows on a Sunday, there was a certain amount, we did just what was necessary. Nothing extra. I don't think John Rayner would hay time either.

It was 1980 that the Rayners started working on a Sunday and they've been doing it ever since.

John Rayner

Nobody worked on a Sunday in me dad's day and me granddad's day. Nobody! We always thought it were awful, one fella Up Dale started on a Sunday, never seen nowt like it.

If you're using horses, do they need a day to have a rest?

They did. That were idea. Give men a rest as well. Now Sunday's like another day. Now there's football and everything going on on a Sunday. We'd no music. Me sister could play piano. That were only instrument we had. When did it start altering? About seventies or so? Going back to my granddad's day they only had neighbours for entertainment. They just came and talked. Stopped to about midnight. One old farmer said he din't like to go to bed same day he got up. He were talking till after midnight! (Laughs) Just talked, didn't they! Tell tales about neighbours.

Jack Haines

When you were hay timing, did the horses have a Sunday off?

No! (Laughs). Well, if we weren't working, they weren't and it just worked like that. But I can't say they had a day off.

John Rayner

They were all Methodist were t' owd Rayners, Up Dale. You've heard of John Wesley haven't ye? Aye. Came on 'orses from Halifax or somewhere. Preaching. And t' owd Rayners used t' be I think Catholics or summat down there, you know in Main Hall, this hall down in reservoir. Yorkes were Catholic, and they were once hiding... what do you call him...? Guy Fawkes ... down in there, cos King Henry was after him. Catholics. From Knaresborough. They were Catholics. Anyway, these owd Rayners, when John Wesley came to Lofthouse, preaching, started building these chapels din't they. There were one at New Houses below Scar, one at Lofthouse, one at Bouthwaite, one at Wath. There were eighteen Methodist chapels round Nidderdale. Now there's only four left. Still one at Wath. And these owd Rayners started preaching as well. And there's a tale, one of them walked to Manchester from Lofthouse to give a sermon. To preach. From Lofthouse to Manchester over hills. He walked. Yeah, he walked, going back to 1750 and that. Over Pennines to Manchester, cos they were spreading this religion, wun't they, Methodists.

In me granddad's day, Wath chapel was on three times a day on a Sunday. Morning, Sunday school in afternoon, and at night. And me dad — they were always short of a Sunday school teacher — he started teking Sunday school in afternoon, and one of pupils said he didn't hear much about Jesus, but he heard plenty about yaus and tups! (Laughs)

Family and Leisure

Jack Haines

Was Sunday ever taken as a special day?

Well, it was for me. You see me mother used t' make us go to Sunday school at Ramsgill and, you know Wath chapel, I had to go there. And you know the anniversary of the chapels? I thought it was most unfair. You had to go up them steps to the pulpit and you either said a piece, whatever it was, which was a piece of poetry, or you sang, and I used to have to do both, and I thought, *This is most unfair!* Cos I was a good singer, you know. I was in the choir at Ramsgill. I could sing.

Connie Bickerdike

Come Sunday, every Sunday the three of us when we were old enough we had t' go to Sunday school. This would be according to the weather, we always went for a walk after Sunday school or we went paddling in the Nidd or my dad use to arrange racing and we used to have sports day on a Sunday afternoon and we had three-legged race and egg and spoon race and sack race. When you go down from Middlesmoor into Stean there was one field that was level and being the only level field we could have all these races and that was always on a Sunday afternoon.

Photo: (Ann Smith)
Family sampler by Ann
Simpson, dated 1896

My mum was a wonderful woman with her hands, crafts and hands craft, knitting, sewing, whatever, but nobody did that on a Sunday and there was a special table cloth came out on a Sunday. When we got back from whatever we'd been doing, walking, or paddling ... that table cloth was on. It was Sunday. But now, what respect does anybody have for a Sunday?

Christine Harker

Me grandma, Eva, she was one of the first members of the W.I. and me granddad's sister was as well. She was Susan Harker. That would be about their only leisure time.

Would they do anything on a Sunday?

Well, obviously on a farm they have to see to the animals, but as far as sewing and things like that, that wasn't classed as being a Sunday occupation. Any sort of sowing or knitting.

And you didn't hang your washing out on a Sunday.

Ooh, no! Well, some people won't do it now. Me mother wouldn't. Just what you're brought up with really, in't it.

Community

Sam Hesselden

Well, Mrs Meredith, she's gone long since, and my wife Pauline, they've all gone, and they were very friendly, and Mrs Meredith said under Any Other Business in the meeting, she said 'I'd like to suggest something...that we start a luncheon club going for people in Wilsill that are by themselves – a man lost his wife or vice versa. They have to be retired.' Well, I thought, 'Oh, my goodness, that'll never get off the ground,' but didn't it. It did that, it went from strength to strength. My wife and her used t' go down there, and do it on a Wednesday once a month. I used t' go and cook meat for 'em and do things like that and set tables up. Well, I were wrong there, I really was.

Now this kitchen, we built a kitchen and we've upgraded it a time or two, new units and such like, new gas cooker – it's all up to date, but two of our members went to get exams for catering. You can't supply hot food if you haven't a licence. So we had t' spend a lot of money in the kitchen, and still it won't meet the regulations required. And they said, 'Well, we'll have to condemn Wilsill chapel because you've t' have two sinks, and you've t' have this and that and other. And we have a toilet – a proper flush toilet with and alarm and a disabled toilet as well – you pull a thing down. And still it won't meet regulations. And they've said, 'There's no insurance if you don't upgrade it again.' Well, it was gonna cost £7000. We're not talking about peanuts. And there's one at Pateley. When they did the furbishing they altered their kitchen and made a dining area and all that what you've seen, and they passed – it's all newly passed regulations. They can do it now at Pateley, and Wilsill couldn't officially. If anybody were poorly after a meal we were in trouble, and dire trouble, so they decided at Pateley, let's move the luncheon club form Wilsill to Pateley. Well, Pateley agreed – 'Yes, come along!' So they closed that down at Wilsill. And it were luncheon club yesterday and I go there whenever I can. And so our little kitchen, new gas cooker only six months syne, and all, aren't what we call Up To Ticket. 'No, you can't serve meals. We can't give you a licence. No, no.' They could nearly close you, you know. It hadn't done us no good.

But I'm glad they've still kept name – Wilsill Luncheon Club – cos it's been going for over thurty years – although it's at Pateley. They can't take no more now until there's a vacancy. If somebody dies, well there'd be a vacancy. I think there's twenty-six about now and it's a good dinner. It's only about four pounds.

My son, he's on the local preacher list and he has been now for quite a many number of years and he can take a sermon. If it's full, it doesn't matter to him. He isn't nervous. He's just happy when he's there anyway. They're getting less because three passed on, and you see you can't replace them. So I don't know what the outlook holds for us. Nobody knows what the future holds for nobody. We don't know. And we just have to go forward and do what's right and straight and that's as far as we can go.

to black [someone] (verb) :
to give them a telling off.

He give us a right good blacking when we were messing about on reservoir.

Rural Voice

Getting
Educated

Photo: (Christine Harker) Lofthouse school 1902

Getting Educated

AN EDUCATION was a way out of the Dale for those who wanted it. Children were taught in small classes in village schools. From there, the cleverest children went to grammar school if their parents let them. The leaving age for pupils slowly rose from 12, to 13, to 14, to 15. Today a young adult must be in some form of education or employment until the age of 18. In the Dale, as people moved to the towns the numbers of children fell and schools combined and closed. Ease of transport has opened up many more opportunities for pupils today.

School

Peter Boddy

I wur in hospital nearly four years during war. At Greenhow school I used a drain pipe, and it turned TB and I wur in hospital nearly four years with it. During war from February 1941 till November '44. I used to ask me mother why I wurn't in a photo at school. She said I were generally poorly when they came to take photos! (Laughs).

You missed a lot of schooling if you were in the sanatorium at Scotton Bank. There wur a school at Scotton. We had t' go there sometimes when we got up, walking about. And a woman came to teach us at Middleton I remember.

When I came out of hospital they started going from school by bus to Pateley cos there weren't so many pupils there then. It got down to five or six when I finished. There didn't seem so many.

I wur eleven when I went in, nearly fifteen when I came out. I didn't bother going to school anymore. Leaving age wur fifteen then I think. So I worked for me father. We used t' go on the moors, dig this gravel, digging fluorspar on the moors past Stump Cross Caverns.

Jack Haines

We moved down to Gouthwaite. Moved down there when I was ten. The bungalow down at Gouthwaite, next to the big house, lived in that for fifty years.

And then we went Pateley school. Hated every minute of it at Pateley. Well, they didn't like anybody from Scar. I'm not telling lies, but that headmaster thrashed me every day. And I mean thrashed me. It used t' be I couldn't hold the pen. I had to go in the porch and put me hand in cold water. And my wife, who ended up head mistress at Pateley, she was in the same class, and she used t' say, 'For Lord's sake, Jack, cry. He wants to make you cry. If you cry for him he'll give up.' I said, 'I aren't crying for him. He can kill me. I aren't crying for him.' He once broke a cane over me. It was hard.

Where was the school?

It's where the school is now, going up Church Bank on the left hand side with the tower, that was where we were. We didn't have school lunches, we took sandwiches, and there were two girls that used t' take the tea – you had t' take your own tea and coffee or whatever – and Eileen and Mary Chalmers they both ended up teachers. No, they weren't happy days at Pateley school.

You met your wife at school.

We were in same class when we were ten. She wur best thing that ever happened to me. Aye, she wur great. She could do anything. You mentioned it, she could do it. Her mother didn't like me. I wonder why...! But she didn't.

Teachers

Audrey Summersgill

My mother was a teacher. She used t' teach at Greenhow school. She lived just down the road here, Brayside. She was an Atkinson. There was quite a few of them. Just one brother. Me mother used t' walk up to Greenhow to the school on a Monday morning and then she used t' stay a couple of nights, two nights, with the headmistress up there, then she'd come back down again on a Wednesday night, then walk back up on Thursday morning. There must've been something special on a Wednesday! (Laughs) And then have Thursday night up there, and then walk back down again on Friday. That's a fair long trek is that! It's all up hill.

She would go up that Moor Houses Road, the little one that goes to False Tooth Bridge as they call it these days.

Is that Peat Lane?

Peat Lane, yes. Then it comes back out on the main road again. It was a fair trot. What time she used to set off I don't know.

That school building is a house now.

It is, yes.

Connie Bickerdike

At school, Miss Ridley was my teacher. Prior to getting into Miss Ridley's room, the school was in two rooms, and the smallest of the rooms was Miss Eglin, and Miss Eglin had a club foot which today they deal with. You were in there I think until you were three or four. It must be four because you don't start until you're three. And then... I can't remember what age you moved down into Miss Ridley's room. And there again, they were happy, happy times. Except on a Wednesday. With being left handed, Billy Slinger who became one of the local gamekeepers, we were made to use our right hand all day Wednesday, which we both hated. It upset me from the start. Going in, I could almost feel sick, and to get something, you know, you write something and it wasn't your work, that was just horrible.

Were you tempted to use your left hand?

Very tempted, but if you did you got the cane. You got a tap on the hand. Miss Ridley was ... she must've had eyes in the back of her head. She was very fond of the cane. Especially towards ... I don't think she liked boys, and if any of them swore, they got their tongue wiped with carbolic soap. Ooh, it was terrible stuff, and it was very pink. Very, very pink. You could smell it everywhere.

On a Monday morning, we always went to school with a penny for the bank. Miss Ridley must've had to deal with that money after school time, wouldn't she?

What did you do with your penny?

We weren't aware of what happened to it. But I've often wondered did the thre'penny bits from the gate opening go into the bank? We were too young. As little ones, if we asked any questions, same as if I'd said to my mum, 'What happens to the pennies?' we were cheeky. We were cheeky.

Lizzie, we were in school together. I think that's when it must have started our friendship because we had desks for two and Lizzie and I were always together at school. We got married in 1946 in October and she was dead in November. Hmm. And we'd been friends all that time. She came to my wedding. I don't know what she died of. She wasn't a physically well girl. There was something very wrong with her which we never found out. She made it to my wedding, happy and normal as usual, and in November we were back up there to her funeral.

You mentioned Miss Ridley and that you kept in touch with her.

Yes. We kept in touch and I can't remember what year it was ... 1956 ... 57 ... It must've been 1957... Miss Ridley came down to us cos we lived in Harrow, Pinner, and Miss Ridley came down to me for a week's holiday because she wanted to see things in London and Windsor and the tourist attractions and I went out with her, whatever she wanted to do depended on her because her eyesight was getting weaker, and whatever there was she wanted me to read it out to her. And at the end of the week she said she'd had a wonderful week's holiday. She was the easiest visitor we ever had. Yeah. And the next I knew, she'd left me in her will. She left me a silver jug, a chest of drawers and various bits of rugs and mats.

She didn't call you Connie, did she?

She would never call me Connie. Constance. It was always Constance. Because Connie was shortening for Constance. And it wasn't. I was christened Connie!

And the letter that arrived telling you about her death...

... It was to Mrs Constance Bickerdike. And there was only ever one person called me Constance. And it was from Heaps, the solicitors at Pateley Bridge. When she retired she lived at a flat in Pateley. Right opposite the Talbot Hotel.

Middlesmoor School 1920

Photo: (Dinah Lee) *from her book* A Stone's Throw From Heaven

Dinah Lee

In your book you talk about the school at Middlesmoor, which isn't there anymore.

No, it's where we had our tea...

...yes, because the house next door is called The...

...The School House. There was a school. There were two classrooms, and the younger children were in the smaller one and the bigger ones were in the larger one. But you see it was from five to fourteen in those days. In two classrooms. And some of the boys were very big and rough — you know how they are. The headmistress, she was called Miss Ridley, and when I look back and think about her, she was very very stern. You daren't hardly breathe. But she had to be. I mean, these big boys, they would have soon been the boss of her if she hadn't. She had to be extremely firm with them, and I know she was very handy with the cane (laughs). But she was a good teacher. She taught everything and all the age groups, although there was someone came in that did have the younger ones at the other end. Two teachers. Yes.

Things were very isolated. You were out on your own in those days. There were very little links with other schools or anything else.

What would you have in the classroom?

When I was there, there was a very large blackboard and it swung — you could swing it over... flip it over. I think there was a radio — I can't remember it much as a child. I can remember it when I was older there. But I can't remember it... I don't think there would be one as a child. There weren't many books. We read the same book over and over again. County supplied library books, and they were in great big boxes, and they would change periodically and we were allowed to choose one of those each to take home, and I loved those because you got a bit more variety. By the time they'd change you'd read all those that were your age group! Yes. I've always enjoyed reading. And these big boxes full of books were a real treasure trove to me.

So, one day there would be a day when all the new books would come.

Yes. It was lovely because you had all these new books to work on. Yes. County supplied those. I think we used to have them for quite a long time. They didn't used to change them very regularly.

And there were two yards. It was split. There was a wall across. And the younger children played in the top one and the older children played in the bottom one. Toilets were outdoors; there's some steps where you went up and the toilets were out there. Girls were at the top and boys were at the bottom somewhere (laughs). Oh! Happy days. I enjoyed my days.

There was a cold water in the porch and that was it. Heating there was coal fires and then we got a stove and that was it. But there were coal fires in both classrooms. Yes. Because you used to keep a good supply of coal, you used to get it to build up for the winter and there was one winter and it was bad and a lot of people... well, the coal man couldn't get up and a lot of people were running low... so school coal came in very handy. People came and used to take a bag. We got it either paid for or a bag in return, but it was there to help people out in the village because otherwise they wouldn't have had anything to heat their homes.

I was happy. I knew everybody. I knew their parents, I knew their children, you knew them before they came to school, and it was just a nice family atmosphere. It was funny at Middlesmoor because my own boys went to school, you see, and then I had my nieces went to school and of course they always called me Aunty Dinah (laughs). All the children in the village called me Aunty Dinah! I'm still Aunty Dinah to a lot of them. They've no relationship at all. They've grown up (laughs). So it's rather nice.

John Rayner (2012)

Liz Palmer, well, she's still up there in Lofthouse. She's modern in't she like. More modern, aye.

Well, she's retired now.

Aye, she has, Liz. Her mum were a Harker. One of them Harkers, her mum. Aye, married a Palmer.

Is Palmer a local name?

No. Last war, Palmer and his dad came from up Durham, you know, working for WarAg – War Agricultural – ploughing fields and that, you know, to grow more food. Government started this scheme. And Palmer and his dad came from up Durham and then got on with this local girl, you see.

Gladys Blakeson (2017)

Did you ever know Elizabeth Palmer?

Was she a teacher?

Yes. Lofthouse teacher.

Is she still alive?

Noo. She died did Elizabeth. Got cancer of the lungs. Ooh, it must be two years since. Time flies. I don't know whether it's two years or three years. She wasn't well at all.

Photo: (Sam Hesselden) Wilsill school

Education

Sam Hesselden

I started at this school, here, Wilsill. This was a school where we are with our depot. Rakes Endowed school. It were a church school. It belonged wi' St Michael and All Angels. Every All Saints Day in Anglicans, the vicar comes and there's a service there in that little church and that's the St Michael's and All Angels and there's a service and all school children have to parade up, file up in twos, and we had t' go to the service. Mind you, we were glad, have a bit of a walk up to church. It were lovely (laughs) and then when service were over, not a long service, but the children of their school, Rakes Endowed, when they finished with the service up there we came back down and carried on with our lessons.

We did our lessons at school. The school teacher were Mrs Pegg. A lady. She were very nice. You know what it's like at school. There was a bell in the Bell House above, like the Church House. It was a big bell. One of the elder pupils he used to climb up onto the roof and he'd scramble on his knees all way across the roof and then he'd start ringing the bell. It were on a little short metal arm – *Ding Ding Ding Ding* – well, she used to come out and ooh she were cross, but she had t' wait while he come down. He had t' come off eventually and of course she gave him a real scalding. So the bell were disconnected then. He couldn't do it anymore.

Nowadays they can't give the pupils the cane because… it changes, rules and regulations. She used t' come, instead of caning some of 'em, she'd hit 'em on side of their head.

'E only lived on Smelthouses this lad and he's like this… he says, 'I'll tell me father!' (Laughs) That's in old language, 'me father'. Course he would do, but 'is dad never came.

How many pupils were there?

At the height, about thurty eight, when I was going.

Gladys Blakeson

My earliest memories is going to school. Me friend at bottom o' yard, she was a bigger girl than me and she used to take me down to school when I was young. And then the line come past… the railway line to Scar came past the playing ground and he used t' blow the whistle. You know Sykes Bank…? Where the big hedge is, that house, and you come up it, this bank. There was a railway went up the bottom you see and a bridge and as he were crossing the main road he used t' have t' come across the main road where that iron bridge is going up to that farm, West House, and it went up the valley at the side of the river and then over another little bridge near Lofthouse. That's where the railway went. And then, you know where the Station House is at Lofthouse, well there used t' be a big boiler thing there and he used t' stop and fill up with hot water, and then the line came out at the end and over that bit of a bridge and then into Scar where the gate is. Up that way. The side of the road was the railway line. There was the main road, then like a banking in't there. And that's where the railway was.

What do you remember about the school?

What do I remember about the school? Well, there was only two classes. One was a lady, a teacher called Miss Houseman, used to take us tiny ones, and then as you got bigger you went into the other one and that was a teacher called Miss Hey. She used t' lodge at the old vicarage at Lofthouse. And then eventually they built some council houses and she got one of those.

Dinah Lee

You were schooled at Middlesmoor?
I went to school at Lofthouse first. I was born in Stean – so I haven't moved far, have I! (Laughs) And I walked to Lofthouse school until I was nine and my father died when I was three and my step brother continued farming but he never enjoyed it and then we moved to Middlesmoor to be with my grandmother and so I went to Middlesmoor school after that, latterly, and then I went to High school. I was a weekly boarder, which was nice. We used to go on a Monday morning and come back on a Friday night. So, it was good because you had the best of both worlds. You still had your home life and your home links as well as being away.

Now, my boys they had to board and they went to the Ripon Grammar school, but they weren't allowed home except half term and once in between. They weren't allowed home for weekends. In some ways you lost the link with them and you weren't able to be as interested in what they were doing as if they'd been gone for the week. But, I mean, it worked out alright. It did them good in the end! (Laughs).

Gladys Blakeson

I never passed an exam to go anywhere. They did say that I should go to art school. I used t' like painting and that you see, and drawing, and Grandma says, 'I can't afford to send you to no art school,' so I never got there.

Dinah Lee

I know she had quite a struggle when I went to the High school you know, with uniform and things like that, but boarding was free, she hadn't t' pay anything for my boarding so that was a help. A taxi used t' come up and take us up to Risplith and then there was a school bus run into Ripon from there. Picked us up, took us to school, and it was the same coming back on a Friday, but there wasn't just me, there was a group of us you see. She would have so much to pay towards this taxi that ran, unless the County provided it, they might have done. I don't know. I can't remember really.

But, I mean, there was... well, there was quite a few of us from Up Dale went. We all went and boarded at Ripon because that was the only way you could get any further education. I had a very different childhood from the ones they have now. They come down every day some of them nowadays. Up Dale now, buses bring the children down. There a bus in the morning. The older children come down.
Are there many children now, up the Dale?
No... well, I'm saying no... the thing is, you see, a farmer up there, they're established. Once they've had their families they stay on very often, so there are no more children coming along the line from many of the farmers. There are more incomers have come into Lofthouse. They've built new houses and there are a few more incomers coming there, but on the whole there are not a lot of children round. There are incomers coming in, they soon settle in I think. But I don't know many of them now. One time I knew them all and I knew the families. I haven't the same links now that I use to have.

John Rayner
Have you heard of Eugene Aram? He murdered somebody. There's a boook written about him. He were a school teacher at Ramsgill and he fell out with somebody, murdered him at Knaresborough, hid him in a cave and then after a few years they found this body and it were him that had murdered him. Eugene Aram. Back in 1880s. There's a boook about it.
Your father would have walked to school?
Yeah, over that wood. There's a road up t' Heathfield through that wood. And there's another in from other side of caravan site. Corn

Close. And they were all miners' kids. Lead miners, up Merryfield Gill. You know where caravan site is, this side there's a lot of lead mines up Merryfield. There were all them kids. Farm kids and that. And there used t' be a school at Ramsgill.

Me dad went t' Heathfield school up there, over that wood there, right up. Me granddad Moses went t' Lofthouse school. They left when they were twelve. Me dad left Heathfield school when he were thirteen and I left when I were fourteen, Pateley school, so there were no education then wur there?

And there were an eleven plus in them days. Have y' heard of that? Eleven plus? Well, I went and sat for it, Ripon Grammar school, me and a friend from Ramsgill – cleverest kids from Pateley school – went t' sit for this eleven plus. Anyway, I passed, but me dad, you see, they were owd fashioned and didn't believe in education, did they, in them days, so I had to stay at home and work. Left when I wur fourteen. Cos they thought if I went there I wouldn't be a farmer, would I? If I got educated I'd have cleared off into towns. There's a song about *Once You See Paris*, or summat in't there (laughs). Yeah! So, that were my education.

nowt (pronoun) :
dialect version of 'nothing'.

Nowt posh, you know (laughs). I have same furniture as me grand-dad had. Table and corner cupboard and sideboard and all that. It's all same, do y' see? It's all same.

Rural Voice

During
The War

Photo: (Peter Boddy) Peter Boddy and his uncle celebrate King George's coronation, 1937

During the War

MANY OF *our narrators were young children during the Second World War.*
Their lives were affected by events at the time as war brought new people in
to the Dale, and took familiar ones out of it.

Gladys Blakeson

I know in war time me grandma use t' say, 'They want some scrap
iron. If you're out walking and you see summat iron off the railway
just pick it up cos they want that.' T' make war things, you see, on
Second World War, so we used t' do! (Laughs) Pick it up and take it
home! It was funny.

What happened to the scrap iron?

Well, they took it and melted it down. You know the village hall at
Lofthouse? There used t' be a nice iron railing all along there because
it was a road that went round to the farm at the other side, and they
took all them. Took 'em all away, cut 'em out, and took 'em away. T'
make ammunition and stuff, wan't it.

School

John Rayner

During war, 1940s I wur at school, a lot of orphans came from Hull.
Bombed it, hadn't they. All little kids in sailor suits. Hundreds of
them. Orphans. Well, I don't know whether they were orphans —
evacuees. Well, they flooded Pateley school. You didn't get much
education, did you, and they were right bad lads. Teacher were giving
'em cane and all that. And they were running away. They parked 'em
in big houses. Eagle Hall — up there, and round about. Teachers
came with them from Hull. Orphans. So there were no education.
Not properly like.

How big would the school have been when you were there?

All kids were there. It doubled in size when they all came.

Was it just lads, or were there some lasses as well?
Aye, both.

Audrey Summersgill
I'm interested in childhood as it would have been and what the town's children had.
I don't know what the town's children used to do. In '39 they built Bewerley Park camp school for evacuees from Leeds. The ones that came to Glasshouses, they lived at Castlestead, they lodged there, then there was another lot up at Eagle Hall, then there was some more up at... they call it The Home of Rest. It's nearly at the start of the second hill as you go up to Greenhow on the right. That's been converted. It's cottages now, or apartments.
Did you mix with the town children much?
No, we didn't go far from the farm. We used to amuse ourselves. There was meself and me sister and me cousin Annie, you see, me uncle's daughter, and we used to go just play together.
Where did Annie and your uncle live?
They lived in the farm house itself and we were up the field.
The only people you'd speak to would be your own family, most of the time?
Mmm, yes.

The Great War

Gladys Blakeson
First World War broke out, and me granddad went to war, and he'd only be a young man then though wouldn't he. I wasn't born then, you see. I wasn't born until 1927. And she got a telegram after about a year to say he's lost presumed killed. And so she thought, *Oh that's it then*, and then after a year he turned up. I think 'e must've been in trenches and not known where he was and he gradually got better you see and he turned up. I says, 'You're lucky you haven't another fella!' (Laughs) Cos she had seven children. Four girls and three boys.

Well Jonny, me youngest uncle, 'e were born after me granddad came back you see. The oldest one went to war with him. There was both his name and his son's name, which was Walter. Walter Williams. As young people, they called him William Williams, me granddad. They both came back. But I don't know what had happened to him, but they sent this telegram, they thought he'd been blown to bits I think, but I don't know where he'd been, and he would never talk about it. Never told us. No. Kept it all to hisself. Very quiet. Very quiet man.

Peter Boddy

During the war, me mother was in the Royal Observer Corps. They had her on the top of the hill... past the church on the left there was a hill, there was Observer Corps place there. Highest hill there. They called it Peter Four. They had to look out for planes coming over during the war, and you had to report it by telephonometer to Leeds. And me dad was in Observer Corps, and he were in ARP first.
Did he serve in the war?
First war. Just after First War he were in army, in Germany to help guard the Rhine or summat. He were born in 1900. He were 18 towards end of First War.

The Second World War

John Rayner

Well, it were forties in war time wurn't it.
Will you have known much of the war while you were here?
Willie Harker, at Raygill House where we got goose, he had to go cos there were three brothers and two stayed at home, and he were captured. German's captured him in France just after D-Day. And so he were away.
He came back?
Yeah, he came back out of prisoner of war camp. And Jack Haines,

he went as far as River Rhine, fighting, and then he got shot in foot or summat so he came back, didn't he. Cos they didn't all come back. It decimated Nidderdale for farmers, cos they had to go. They only allowed one... a dad on a farm, or just one maybe. And then they sent Land Girls.

But you stayed here? Because you're the only boy.

Oh, I were too young, in forties. I were only ten or twelve or fourteen. Too young. But I know a lot of farm lads had t' go. They were older.

Lads that you grew up with.

Mmm, yeah.

Photo: (Christine Harker) A photo of Eva Nicolson for her sweetheart

Christine Harker

Me grandmother (Eva Nicolson) and her step mother had the post office at Middlesmoor and they had the telegraph system, and she had the unfortunate job of delivering the telegrams during the war. *She would see them before the families did.*

Yes. And one lady's son, her only child, they got this telegram through and Lofthouse Post Office didn't have a telegram centre, so it all came to Middlesmoor. And she (Eva) had to go to Lofthouse to tell this lady that her only son had died. But he'd only been in a month and it were measles he died for. He hadn't got out to the front. And when me grandmother got there, his mother couldn't read and write so me grandmother had to read it out to her, and me dad said she always said that was one of the hardest things that she'd ever done. But because they got the news first, they knew when war was over first.

That was telegrammed through?

Yes. And me great grandma got hold of a man in the village who had no idea how to ring a bell cos all the bells had been silenced in war time, so the whole Dale knew. It would be quite ... I mean it gets me every time. Very moving.

It's not like now when you can tell people in an instant.

Sometimes it goes round too quickly today, doesn't it (laughs).

Jack Haines

What was it like coming back from the war?

I was in hospital, you see. I was in three military hospitals. They used to patch you up, and they'd send you back (laughs). And the last one was just outside Hamburg and they flew a lot of us home in Dakotas. Dakota aeroplanes. And we ended up in... it's just outside London... Anyway, we ended up there, so I was in hospital when the war finished.

Sam Hessleden

When we were in Home Guard there wur just one scary time. The authorities, it were night time, and they said, 'Now look 'ere, there's an emergency. There's been some paratroopers dropped – Germans – dropped, you know, from sky, and they're up 'ere on Pateley Moor.' Well, we got up there to Pateley Moor and it wasn't on Pateley Moor. They were nowhere in our section. I don't know what I'd have done if I'd have seen them (laughs)! Oh dear! We've had some real good times, but we've had some uneasy times.

We had a German prisoner of war working for us when war was on and me dad had a farm and he worked for me dad. There's somebody arranged it all and he lived in with me mother and dad on a farm. Hanz they called him. Hanz. And he stopped wi' me dad until war were finished and he didn't want t' go back.

Well, we set him on a tractor. Me brother and me we were very very busy and we set him on tractor. We said to me dad, 'Can you lend us your man?' and he said, 'Well, yes.' Well, we set him on just up Blazefield at top of hill – it's only a stone's throw away. At end of this field there were a bit of a slack hollow. Well it were bigger than you think because he came along and it tippled him. He turned it over. When it went over he had a set of big disc harrows at back, he were getting land ready for seeding. They were one with a pin you see and it all went over together and it fastened him in where mudguard is. Poor fella. He got out. He were thin enough for nowt t' hit him, t' block him in.

Oh, we've had all sorts. All sorts.

Jack Haines

I have many memories. Some I don't want to remember about the army.

See that belt there...? Not the leather... The buckle were on the Somme. Found on the Somme. First World War. We often wonder who was in it when he was killed.

Then there was the aeroplane went into the reservoir. I was going up the side of the reservoir in a Land Rover and they'd been at it for a while – they were both jets – passing low over the reservoir. And they would never talk about it afterwards, but there was a little micro-light and the one that was at the bottom as you came out, this micro-light was in front of it and he tipped and his wing just touched the water and it cartwheeled, and there were a young lad there about twelve, so I sent him down to Mrs Longster's at Gouthwaite Hall. I said, 'You've seen as much as I've seen. Ring in and tell 'em what you've seen and you want the services out to see to it.' And off he went. And I went round as fast as I could and all there was was two pools of oil on the top and a map case.

Anyway the first things to arrive were local police, and credit to them, one of them stripped off and in he went. 'I can't see owt,' he says, 'There's only oil and this map case.' Well, we were always taught in the forces you look after your own because they've got to look after you. Helicopter came and I thought, *This is it... divers and what have you. Nurses.* Nurses... they stood round chattering and talking. Anyway it was a bloody farce, to be quite honest, it really was. We went up to Scar and got a boat to go out in a boat to see if there was anything. Eventually some divers arrived. They'd got no air in their bottles. It's unbelievable, in't it? Anyway, they went in and they found him. And he's still strapped in his seat. And I said, 'Well, for God's sake get him out!' 'What with?' 'Well, you've got them big knives, cut the straps and let him out.' 'Oh no, we can't do that. We might fire the ejector seat.' Anyway, some more landed and they went down. What did they do? Fire the ejector seat. Lost him again. What a bloody farce it was.

Got him out eventually. The thing that was really good was the crew that came to get the aeroplane out. They went down and put these bags round it and then they filled it with air, floated it to top. And I got a smashing letter from Chief Constable: *Thank you for your public service on the day*, and I got a lovely letter from his widow saying 'thank you' for trying to help him. And I've lost them now. I don't know where they are.

And from the office they said, 'How much fuel is there in this plane for polluting the river?' so I went to one of these offices and asked how much fuel there was. They said 'How do I know!?' I said,

'I beg your pardon, you must have known how much fuel you had when you set off. You must know how long he'd been flying, so you must have a good idea about how much fuel is in the plane.' And it was a right breezy day, so as it came up it was blowing off, you know, evaporating. They didn't seem to know anything. For long enough up at Lossiemouth, up in Scotland, they swore they didn't have a plane missing. I said, 'I saw it go in! There's an aeroplane in there.' 'Oh no, you're mistaken sir.'

How can you miss it, an aeroplane?

And what made me laugh... well, it were nowt to laugh about... there was a lad sat on the arches in Gouthwaite fishing. And he said, 'Well, I knew nobody was going to bother with me with all that lot going on so I went and did a bit of fishing.'

while (preposition) :
until.

We went dancing up there and the band never came... they'd been in pub... and they didn't come in and play while ten o'clock. You'd be waiting a good hour. But instead of finishing at one o'clock, nine while one, they played while three.

Rural Voice

Dancing
Years

Photo: (Gladys Blakeson) Lofthouse Silver Band

Dancing Years

IT WASN'T all work in the Dale. The young people enjoyed music, drinking and dancing at regular events. Some local musicians played at home, at church, or at concerts to raise money for charities. Others played in dance bands that gained a reputation for their drinking as much as for their music.

San Hesselden

We used t' have little concerts, you know, down 'ere. Wi' people play. Do you know Sam Cryer at Warsill? He were mayor of Harrogate were Sam Cryer. Well, he had a organ, an electric organ you could carry about. They've even made 'em smaller and they've made 'em lighter. These were as big as those drawers there. And he would play.

Now, he got together a group... *Sam Cryer and Party*, that's what they called it. He used t' go round and play at harvest times... (chuckles). But I've done it for donkeys' years (chuckles)... and especially me wi' (chuckles)... you're never gonna believe this... I learnt t' play the violin when I were twenty. I should've tried t' learn it when I were only eight or ten. And I played violin for Sam Cryer and his party (laughs).

Kerry David... he lives here. He's main architect at Pateley. He's a proper architect. We're fortunate to have him in village. He's unique. He's a master of all that. He's done a lot of planning. Building hospitals... everything that a hospital needs, it requires... he knows. But you see, he's like everybody else, getting older. Now, he had a violin, and so me and him got together (laughs). We went down to... (laughs)... Him and me and David Barker, 'e were minister up 'ere, he played piano for us. And Kerry's wife now plays organ herself and she's very good at it. She's an organist now at Pateley. Well, Kerry and me, they wanted us to give 'em a performance down 'ere. This place were full and we played for an evening... it were for charity. We did everything for charity, mostly Children in Need and such as that. Helen Keller. Children for the blind and all that.

(Laughs) I still like it. I used t' play for my wife Pauline and all that, and my friend Stanley were a good player on piano, Stanley was, and him and me, we'd go into there, and Pauline and Nancy, our wives, they were sat in there, this was a Sunday, and we'd play... oh, we'd go through all sorts... They wanted us to go again, but my fingers... can just get hold of it. It's arthritis, and I think it's time I put my violin away.

You do do a lot in a life time.

Gladys Blakeson

We used to have a dance band, you know. Three brothers. One played the piano or a squeeze box, the other one was the drummer, and the other one played the saxophone. That's the Coates brothers. And then our band master, he played the trumpet, and this photo is one of the dances, fancy dress dances, and there's my cousin and me aunt on it, and me husband.

Photo: (Gladys Blakeson) Fancy dress dance with Coates brothers' band behind.

That's the band at the back on the stage. Those men sat at the back here is some of the band, you see. Coates. *Midnight Follies* they used t' call theirselves. *Midnight Follies*. And many a time they didn't start banding till midnight! They'd stop in pub playing darts and then they'd come and everybody would cheer because they'd landed.

John Rayner

Lofthouse Band, brass band, there were four brothers – Coates – they could play any instrument without music, without looking at it, and maybe about eight farmers and four Coates. About a dozen of them, and they went all down Pateley, right up top of street, came back down and round. Everywhere. And they did all of Nidderdale, right up to New Year's Eve. And they were once at top of Pateley and they gave them all a drink didn't they... every house you went to you got a drink, in Pateley. They weren't Methodists, were they. They got sort of half drunk, way up b' new chapel, top of street, so they left him. And two hours later, local policeman was stood at bottom of street and Harry Metcalfe came staggering down street, and he said to local policeman, 'Have you seen anything of a band?' (Laughs) They were away home! Aye. It were funny were that, wan't it? He didn't say, 'Have you heard one?' He said, 'Have you *seen* owt of a band?' Cos they allus ended up drunk did Lofthouse Band. And it sounded beautiful, carols outside. It sounded beautiful when you looked through window.

Sam Hesselden

We used to go up to Lofthouse to dance, and *Midnight Follies*... have you ever heard of them? There were three... all brothers... Coates. There were Billy Coates, he played piano all by ear, no music, but he could make that piano talk. And another one on trumpet or something. And another on drums. And occasionally another man with them on trombone or saxophone. Well, they liked to drink. They used t' be always in pub.

This were back a lot of years. The Dale has changed a lot, like every-where else. If you were at a whist drive it would start about seven o'clock and at half past eight or nine o'clock we start dancing. Well, they didn't come. I took my wife up there. When we were married, 1960 that were, we went dancing up there and the band never came... they'd been in pub... and they didn't come in and play while ten o'clock. You'd be waiting a good hour. But instead of finishing at one o'clock, nine while one, they played while three. Because they'd been in pub before they'd come, and then had another little drink and all this... They used to be late in starting, but they'd give it y' other end.

Well, we came out of there once at three o'clock one morning and we could see... it were bright were sky... Aurora Borealis were on. Northern Lights. I'd never seen them before and I've never seen them since. But, oh, how glorious they were. It just lit all of sky up and it were like a big, massive... It wasn't a round thing, it was shaped more like a square, and the colours... you could hardly credit it. It wur beautiful, it were. It'd be four o'clock when we got down here to Wilsill and they were still on but we could only see half of them. Now we drove up this hill, up the Rakes, ont' Ripon Road, as high as you can get, you can look down towards Thirsk and all that flat area, Ripon and all there, and light were very big. Oh, they were beautiful. Absolutely gorgeous. We've had some doings, I'll tell you.

They were the Dancing Years. And they were lovely. They were really, really lovely.

Dinah Lee

You mentioned a step brother.

I had a much older step brother. He was much older than me. Well, family came out of Swaledale and his mother died after they came into Nidderdale and his father married my mother, but he was quite a bit older. George was always a part of my life because with losing my own father, not having a father, he was always sort of there, and he was an excellent pianist and an organist, and he used to play all round at Dos in the Dale.

Gladys Blakeson

Got me sunhat on in this photo with me instrument.
Which instrument do you play in the band?
Tenor Horn. That's a better one, in me uniform. That's a tenor horn.
Been in it fifty-two years. Since I've had me stroke I think I'll pack it
up. I'll be eighty-nine in September, so... I don't know whether to
pack it up or not. I feel I've lost a lot because I haven't been there
since April, since I had me stroke, and I feel the music they're playing
now I wasn't there to learn it, you see. You learn different music
when you go on a Thursday night. Then they used t' go to Lofthouse.
Well they've packed Lofthouse up now. I don't know why he has.
He took the job on as band master and now he's decided he wants
to play and doesn't want to conduct, and of course the people were
getting less and less. There's only about eight people.

Sam Hesselden

I play it sometimes on a Sunday morning now. Stephen's getting
ready and he's singing upstairs to me playing hymns what we might
be going to have. You can't hardly credit it. It were lovely. I used to
go with Sam Cryer. We went all over the place. We went to Leeds,
but that were heavy going... proper stage and all that, but people were
just like ice (laughs). We couldn't make 'em laugh. Elsewhere we've
been... up above Middlesmoor, and Ripon we've been a few times.
And Summerbridge and... we play a selection of three at a time. They
clap and clap and clap.

I've enjoyed them. Called them Dancing Years. Cos we were in
dancing clubs. We could go to a dance, and dances started at eight
o'clock while one and we'd do thurty-two dances all in that time.
We were still ready for work next morning at half past seven. Never
late for work. Such a lovely... A man playing piano, when it were live
music, a man on drums, and a man on violin.

thee (pronoun) :
archaic or dialect form of 'you'.

Tom Bradley. You've heard of them talk of Tom Bradley, have thee?

Rural Voice

Lets Talk about the Locals

Photo: (John Rayner) Gathering to watch the sheep washing, 1914

Let's Talk about the Locals

AN OPPORTUNITY to talk about the local characters is not to be missed.
Before television and telephones, people had neighbours for entertainment,
staying until late into the night talking and telling stories. Here our narrators
share a few tales about some of the people who stick out in their minds.

Let's Talk about Mr Renton

Jack Haines

He were a funny old fella were Renton. He always knew when me
mother were baking at Scar. She always made him one of those little
brown loaves. He always knew which day it was to go to Scar. Him
and me dad started within a week of one another, when they were
first building Scar back in the twenties, well, nineteen hundred or
whatever it wur. Aye. And they always got on well together. I was
born at Scar and owd Renton wanted me to go and work there then
when I left school at fourteen.

And owd Renton shouted, 'Jack Haines, come 'ere!' There were
all these so-called toffs, you know. And he says, 'Now, listen, this is
Jack Haines,' he says, 'this is one of my men. This is one of the only
men that's any bloody good,' he said.

We once had a fella wanted me to fill a pipe in the Ramsgill syphon
in half an hour. I said, 'No.' He said, 'I've told you to fill it in half an
hour.' I said, 'I know what you've told me, but I aren't doing it. It takes
two hours to fill that syphon and that's what it's gonna take.' Well, he
rambled on and rambled on. I said, 'Let's go down and talk to Renton.'
There were no mobile phones then. Had to walk down to Ramsgill to
telephone. Could've had it filled b' time we'd faffed about. He said,
'He won't be at office.' I said, 'No, but he'll be at home and I've got his
number.' So he talks to Renton, and Renton says, 'Put Jack on.' And
he says, 'What's matter, Jack?' I said, 'He wants this syphon filling in
half an hour and I won't do it.' 'How long do you say?' 'I say two hours.'

'Well, listen, I'll tell you this Jack Haines: if you blow the syphon up it won't be his fault, it'll be yours, so you do it your way.'

Let's Talk about Mr Campbell

Gladys Blakeson

I'm gonna see if I've got that picture. There's some old folks here. That's me grandmother on there, and an uncle, and the landlord that was here fer rent. And lots of people hadn't a photograph of him. They keep saying, 'Campbell Houses.'

The chap with the bowler hat and the pipe?

Yes. They called him Campbell. And when I was fourteen, he gave me this prayer book. You undo it and inside he's wrote in it.

That's a beautiful colouring on the outside.

Mmmm. He's wrote. That's the man.

'Presented to Gladys Williams, Chapel Walk, Lofthouse in Nidderdale by Frederick Sinclair Campbell, Ashfield, 9th October 1941 Pateley Bridge'. It's The Book of Common Prayer. What a beautiful thing. The edges are gold. You'd need good eyesight to read this.

I was only young then, wan't I? Fourteen I think, or thirteen.

Photo: (Gladys Blakeson) Gladys Blakeson's grandmother and uncle with landlord, Mr Campbell

Let's Talk about Mrs Knowle

Gladys Blakeson

That's me as a postwoman, look. That's when we were told we were made redundant. He's got boots on, she's got wellies on, and I've got running pumps on! (Laughs) I used t' walk up and run like mad back down the hill.

How old were you when you finished working as a postwoman?

Well, that was 1947... no, 1974... I got it wrong way round. 1974 when I were made redundant.

Mrs Knowle that lived right at the top of the edge of the moor, the highest farm there is, it's sort of in between Stean and where the

Photo: (Gladys Blakeson) Gladys (centre) as post woman

caravan site is, right on edge of moor... there was allus a cup of tea. A cup of tea at bottom and a cup of tea at top. She said to me one morning, 'I've got a little bedroom upstairs I want light papering. D'you think you could paper it for me?' I says, 'Yes, I'll come back. Paper it.' So I did. I had to walk all way back again to paper this bedroom. Mmm (laughs).

Photo: (Christine Harker) Fred Harker and his parents at Stean

Let's Talk about Fred Harker

Connie Bickerdike

I remember Fred Harker... He was such a good looking boy. He stood out from all the others. Fred Harker. He was a real good looking lad.
Did you play with him as a child?
No. We didn't mix much with people further down the valley. I think at the time he lived in Lofthouse.
...which is actually only about a mile away, or two, from where you lived.
Oh yes.

Let's Talk about Tom Bradley

Gladys Blakeson

Tom Bradley. You've heard of them talk of Tom Bradley, have thee?
I haven't, no.
Well, he used to have Lofthouse pub, and How Stean Gorge. It went
with the pub cos it all belonged John Smith you see.

Let's Talk About Uncle John

John Rayner

He had a shop in Ripon, Uncle John, for years. 'John Rayner Gentle-
man's Outfitters'. And it were down North Street. And when he died
he left it t' lad worked in shop and he had t' keep saying name of it.
But it's gone now. It were there up to ten or twenty years ago. Aye.

Let's Talk About Jane Whitfield

Connie Bickerdike

In The Temperance Hotel, Jane Whitfield, one of the daughters of the
owners, went nursing, which was something I always wanted to do. And
when she was going to the hospital to start her training, everything had
to have name tapes and I was instigated to go and help. And when I
was stitching these labels on, I thought, 'Ooh, I wish it was me.' Yes. I
was quite envious of her going. But I did follow (laughs).

Let's Talk About Mr Watson

Gladys Blakeson

We used to go as children to watch Mr Watson milk the cows, and
he used t' say, 'Oh, you're here again!' and laugh and joke with us.

And then, he was sat milking away, and all at once he'd turn it and squeeze it to soak us. We used t' go purposely, cos we knew he'd do it! (Laughs) He used t' drench us with milk!

Let's Talk About Owd Tom

John Rayner

You grew your own hay. In them wet hay times it were a disaster. In me granddad's diary in 1890 and 1900 an Irish man came. Me grandma said he were once here for a month... he came at first of July for hay time, this Irish man. 'Owd Tom' they called him... and one year it rained every day for that month. It meant Tom cleared off, didn't he? Went down harvesting. He never did nothing for a month! They'd have to pay him. It rained solidly for a month. It were a disaster, like. Aye. First thing he did, he sharpened his scythe and he mewed lawn out there to see if it was sharp.

They Were All Characters In A Way

Connie Bickerdike

Everybody knew everybody.
Where there any characters that stand out in your mind?
Both the shop keepers... they were so different. Eglin, who was a relative of Dinah's, Mr and Mrs Carling, she was a big, fat lady (laughs). And Mrs Walker in the other shop, she was just the opposite... very thin. And after we'd left Middlesmoor, my younger brother was very very friendly with Stanley. That was the Walker's son. But he's no longer with us.

I think they were all characters in a way! (Laughs)

starved (adjective) :
cold.

She'll be starved, that girl (wearing a small mini dress)

Rural Voice

Get Up
And Go

Photo credit: Gladys Blakeson outside her home, Middlesmoor

Get Up and Go

A FINAL WORD from Gladys Blakeson.

That's probably a good time to finish, Gladys. That's been lovely hearing you talk...

Mmm. Different things that's happened...

... yes. I liked the description of your grandmother cooking and baking.

Ah, yes (laughs). Well, time's flown when you think about it. I can't believe I'm that age I am. Can't believe it. Because the things that's happened in them years, you wouldn't have thought, in my time, would y'.

How do you feel inside? Do you still feel the same as you did when you were younger?

What d'you mean?

Well... because... you get older, don't you. Your body gets older.

Yes, your bodies get older. Well, with a stroke it knocked me back a bit, but I just feel as I want to get up and go.

You've always been like that?

Yes, always.

Rural Voice

Glossary

BELOW IS a selection of words used in Nidderdale and their local meanings as explained by the narrators. Most of the words are taken from the text of this book, and some were discussed in later conversations after the recordings were made.

back end (noun) : latter part of the season.
Up Swaledale, they can't start mowing meadow way into July and sometimes it starts raining all back end, don't it.

beater (noun) : (1) a person who beats the flames during controlled burning of the moors. (2) a person who drives the game birds from the undergrowth into the open.
(Context 2) The beaters are the ones who are actually moving, and they're beating their flags to get the grouse to move.

beating (verb) : (1) regulating the spread of fire on the moorlands during controlled burning by beating out fires. (2) the action of driving the game birds out into the open.
There's two sorts of beating. There's beating of the fires, and there's ... beating of the birds.

to black [someone] (verb) : to give them a telling off.
He give us a right good blacking when we were messing about on reservoir.

brossen (adjective) : over full.
He'll be brossen after eating all that.

butt (noun) : a low barrier, usually of sods or peat, behind which the 'Guns' stand to shoot game.
There's a line of shooting butts there and they flag the grouse towards the butts.

byre (noun) : cow shed (also called mistal).

copper (noun) : a large copper or iron container for boiling laundry.
We used to have the copper on boiling there.

cratch (noun) : a long open trough or rack used for holding food for farm animals out of doors.
We used to have the pig on a big cratch and it were put on there and then you scalded it and scraped all the hair off with these old fashioned candlesticks.

cripple hole (noun) : a small hole in a stone wall that can be opened or closed to let sheep through.
We used to get more sheep from other moors when we gathered than there is on now all together, till we got it fenced. In our case, there's a cripple hole straight out of pen into our field, but rest of the farmers walked their sheep home.

drive (verb, also noun) : to chase game birds from cover into the open.
You try to take out what we call a 'drive' with the wind so the beaters would line right out around here, with what we call 'flankers' on each side, three or four on each side.

flank (flanker) (noun) : the edge of a drive of game birds (a person at the edge of a drive of game birds) controlling the side of the formation.
You've got to think of the public, and you set your flank out so that when anybody appears on the footpath the flag goes up and shooting stops.

foot cock (noun) : at hay time, a small pile of hay.
The little ones we used to make were foot cocks. If it was just in bits of rows you got your rake and you sort of fetched a bit over like that and did it with your foot that way, and that was your little foot cock.

gievelock (noun, spelling uncertain) : crowbar.
We'd say, 'Go an' get the gievelock to get this cow shifted,' to stop cows sitting down for too long.

to gowd (verb) : to clip the sheep's tails before putting them to the tup.
We'll be gowding sheep tomorrow.

green top : milk delivered in glass milk bottles were sealed with foil lids, with the lid colour showing what sort of milk it contained. Silver top was full fat pasteurised. Silver and red striped was semi skimmed. Green top was farm fresh bottled.
It was called fresh farm bottled in those days. We still got it – green top – when we came down here.

the Guns (noun) : the sportsmen and sportswomen who shoot game.

han't (dialect) : haven't, hasn't, hadn't.

jockey (noun) : at hay time – a loose arrangement of hay in the fields. Larger than foot cocks and smaller than pikes.

...when it was getting nearly ready but not quite, and it was going to rain, you made jockeys. They were quite substantial really but you didn't trample them down or anything. You just made them with a fork and put the last bit on upside down so it shed the rain off a bit.

to lamp (verb) : hunt at night using lamps, in this case for foxes.

We lamp the fox at night. A lamp on top of the vehicle with a handle inside. One person is driving the vehicle and another person is doing the lamp. You find the fox, and if it's safe you dispatch them with a high powered rifle, and you spend a lot of time on that, especially at night.

lear (noun) : barn.

A Rayner family story tells that Shakespeare visited Gouthwaite farm, and took the name for King Lear from the name of their barn, 'High Lear'. The barn is known today as 'High Barn'.

mistal (noun) : cow shed (also called byre).

I can remember them milking by hand when I was little. There were two mistals ... there'd be ten cows either side and then a little one of six.

navvy (noun) : a labourer working on a building site, excavation, etc... Shortened from *navigator*.

There were a lot of navvies, or people, working at Scar ... They were people that came to work when they were building Scar, and they were people, very often Irish, who used to travel from these building areas. They used to go from one to another. That's how they made a living. And then they would send their wages back to their families in Ireland.

nowt (pronoun) : dialect version of 'nothing'.

Nowt posh, you know (laughs). I have same furniture as me granddad had. Table and corner cupboard and sideboard and all that. It's all same, do y' see? It's all same.

over the tops : the (usually more direct) route over the high moors between dales.

Me grandfather ... and a lad called Harry Graham worked together all over, they walked over the tops started work at Scar, from Leighton over the moor.

owd (adjective) : dialect version of 'old'.

In me granddad's diary in 1890 and 1900, an Irish man came. He came at first of July for hay time, this Irish man. 'Owd Tom' they called him.

owt (pronoun) : dialect version of 'anything'.

You modern lasses, you don't know owt about things like that!

pike (noun) : hay stack. In Northern English dialect, 'pike' is a pointed or conical hill. The hay stacks take their name from this shape.
Then we made pikes... You used to stand on those and build them round yourself. You'd keep filling the middle up. They were like haystacks.

pike bogie (noun) : a small wheeled base on which to transport the hay pikes.
Then you had a pike bogie. It was just like a flat trailer with iron wheels on it and it was held down with a thing at the front, a pin through, and when you got to your pike you backed it up and if you had somebody with you, you pulled the front up a bit, generally with the horse, like, so far under the pike, then you got a big thick rope which was always used for tug of war in tug of war competitions.

to play pop (verb) : not quite being cross with you, but getting that way.
I always used to be helping where I could, and me mother used to play pop with me carrying buckets of chopped turnips across the big yard there to some animals that were tied up.

to row (verb) : at hay time, to rake the hay into rows in the field.

starved (adjective) : cold.
She'll be starved, that girl (wearing a small mini dress)

to snig (verb) : to drag along the ground by a chain or rope fastened at one end. Used in the context of collecting hay pikes from the fields.
Farm man used t'come, 'Are we sniggling pikes today?' he used to say. Sniggling! Instead of snigging.

to sniggle (verb) : local corruption of 'snig'.

to strew (verb) : at hay time, scattering the cut grass in the field to help it dry.
Women all helped in them days out in fields, strewing about.

thee (pronoun) : archaic or dialect form of 'you'.
Tom Bradley. You've heard of them talk of Tom Bradley, have thee?

tup (noun) : male sheep used for mating with the ewes.
Fella from Derbyshire bought this fifty thousand pounder, and if that tup on some good sheep gets a few tups worth ten thousand each, he's got his money back, hasn't he.

to turn (verb) : at hay time, turning the cut grass over in the fields to help it dry.
We did some hay timing. Turning and strimming and rowing, all these jobs. With the rake.

wan't (dialect) : weren't, wasn't.
I was only young then, wan't I? Fourteen I think, or thirteen.

while (preposition) : until.
We went dancing up there and the band never came... they'd been in pub... and they didn't come in and play while ten o'clock. You'd be waiting a good hour. But instead of finishing at one o'clock, nine while one, they played while three.

wrecken (noun) : the hook for hanging the kettle on beside a fireplace.
Me mother allus put kettle on wrecken first thing in morning.

yau (noun) : local pronunciation of 'ewe', a female sheep.
And me dad started teking Sunday school in afternoon, and one of pupils said he didn't hear much about Jesus, but he heard plenty about yaus and tups!

Rural Voice

Index of photographs

Rural Voice

Acknowledgements

There are many people to thank for this book being created. A great deal of thanks goes to the narrators who allowed me into their lives to share their stories and their photographs. Also to those who passed on names and suggested stories and kept me moving forwards on the path. Thanks go to the Nidderdale Area of Outstanding Natural Beauty for the use of some of the stories that I collected when I volunteered for their Moorlands Project. To Karen Griffiths, Interpretation Officer at the Yorkshire Dales National Park Authority, for the use of her saying. To Louis de Bernières for the use of his poem, The Old Ones. To the Friends of AONB Countryside Fund for funding the printing both of this book and of the accompanying audio CD. To the members of the Thursday writing group for your support, and for proof reading the text - Aileen, Andy, David B, David McA, Kathryn, Linda, Maxine. To my friends for their support and encouragement. And with love to Mel, and to Phil.